# CROWD

Volume 1, Issue 1
Fall/Winter 2001

Front cover photograph "Untitled" by Matthew Monteith © 2001

"Grenada, Winward Islands, Aug 1999" published courtesy of "5eme Etage-Paris, France" © 2001

"The Trees are Down" and "Fame" published courtesy of Carcanet Press, U.K. © 2001

Paintings by Richard Prince published courtesy of the Barbara Gladstone Gallery.

Artwork by Joe Brainard and Ron Padgett appears courtesy of the Tibor de Nagy Gallery,
with permission of the Joe Brainard Estate.

"Nerve" is excerpted from *Melancholy of Anatomy* by Shelley Jackson,
to be published by Anchor Books in 2002.

"The Buried Boy" is excerpted from *Good as Any* by Timothy Westmoreland,
to be published by Harcourt Trade Publishers in January 2002.

"Follen Street" will appear in *Small Gods of Grief* by Laure-Anne Bosselaar,
to be published by BOA in 2001.

"Lucy, I'm Home!" will appear in *Lanscape with Human Figure* by Rafael Campo,
forthcoming in Spring 2002 from Duke University Press.

All design by ADM's Design Machine.

CROWD is published biannually by Crowd Magazine, 119 North 11th Street 1A, Brooklyn, NY 11211.
For information write to the above address, email info@crowdmagazine.com
or visit our Web site: *www.crowdmagazine.com*.

ISSN 1536-5298
ISBN 0-9713348-0-3

EDITORS
Aimee Kelley
Lily Saint

ART EDITOR
a.c. chapman

FICTION EDITORS
Jason Brody
Luis Jaramillo

PHOTOGRAPHY EDITORS
Eric Leshinsky
Katherine Wolkoff

POETRY EDITOR
Tanya Rubbak

ASSOCIATE EDITORS
David Grosz
Catherine Luttinger
Danielle Pafunda

ADVISORY BOARD
Dorothy Allison
Aimee Bender
Gail Boyajin
D. A. Powell
Martha Rhodes
David Trinidad

# CONTENTS

## POETRY

# FICTION

# ART

# Aimee Kelley & Lily Saint
## A Letter from the Editors

*CROWD* exists to unite urban, creative output in one magazine. In addition to mixing painters, poets, photographers and fiction writers in *CROWD*, we are pleased to pair unknown writers and artists with their more established contemporaries. A number of pieces in this debut issue highlight genre-crossovers: Joe Brainard and Ron Padgett collaborated to create wry social commentary through humorous collage; Jane Hammond's series of paintings are based on titles suggested by poet John Ashberry; "Personal Monuments" explores an individual's relationship to the physical monuments of a city through writing and photography; Robert Archambeau's poem "Two Short Films" imagines Wordsworth and Marinetti in film while Richard Prince explores the use of text in painting. Forthcoming issues will continue to explore the implications of multi-genre art through dialogue between artists and writers. We hope you enjoy our first issue as much as we enjoyed putting it together.

*The Editors*

# Robert Archambeau

## Two Short Films on the translation of the European imagination to America

. . . what we feel of sorrow and despair
From ruin and from change, and all the grief
The passing shews of being leave behind,
Appeared an idle dream . . .
                    Wordsworth, *The Prelude*


Up to now literature has exalted a pensive immobility, ecstasy, and sleep. We intend to exalt aggressive
action, a feverish insomnia . . .
                    Marinetti, *Futurist Manifesto*


### 1. Wordsworth at the Cuyahoga's Mouth

In newsreel stock, in jumpy monochrome
You mount the windy bluff, glance back and turn
To face the valley. Far below, white water foams

Birds cry, and black waves peel from slabs of rock,
Back down to the great lake's boom and suck.
You stand, a silhouette, black coat and stick.

The film moves quickly now—clouds fly and light's
A flickered blur of days and nights. You wait,
The still point of a world that's turned to haste.

You wait, and plowed lines break the dark earth's crust—
The valley peopled now—and frontier huts
Crop up each harvest time. A rail line thrusts

On past that limestone ridge, with quick faint wraiths
That, caught in a frame that stutters through the gate,
Are horses, wagons, wide-backed men. You wait,

Brick chimneys frame the screen and black smoke swells,
A furnace-city churns its molten steel—
And one quick night's a flash: city plays hell.

And you, above this growth and flux and ruin,
Does your sleepwalker-muse fetch Whitman songs
*Great port, great ore-port, great handler of iron—*

Or bring *an image of tranquility*
*So calm and still*, a green dream's tapestry
Of soft grass overgrowing history?

I can't expect an answer: You stand, there,
And breathe the flickered light of setting suns, the living air.


## 2. Marinetti at Union Station, Chicago

Arrived, the locomotive paws the track,
deep-chested, bellowing

(we gather, from this silent reel);
its steam-plumes jet in cavern air

beneath the city. And, arrived—
in the city of railyards,

apparatus, of stokers groping blackened
through the mill-fire's angry blast,

the city of shipping, chemical manufacture,
stockyards blazed with electric moons—you,

mounting the platform, gestures broad,
erratic, oratorical.

Saying (we barely see, white letters
over faded stock) *Hold no ideal mistress high,*

*her form divine rising to touch clouds*;
saying *All must be swept aside,*

*to express our whirling life of steel, of pride,*
*of fever and exalted speed;*

saying, in that rush of sailors, workmen,
quick-eyed thieves, *death to Ciceroni, antiquarians. . .*

Mechanic-limbed and darting, the crowd
won't pause to hear you, and I

wonder, do you dream of Venice,
soft, past-loving, shocked

in all her statuary, when you declared
*The first dawn is now, an explosive breath*?

You, erratic, oratorical, the last frame
fading on your words, *our bodies die for speed*

*for movement and for darting light.*

# John Beer

## SARAJEVO

The houses of the dead come in a variety of colors,
though none I can describe:
red, blue, reddish-blue, purple.
One boot grows sleepy and withers.

For these and other reasons, the ice dancers
are no longer found at the practice rink.
No wonder my bottles are dank,
fettered with marjoram and a thin layer of silt.
Friendly as a mailman, the war machine
putters along. I can wear that blouse now.
It's a starry night like any other.

So I have called you into this clearing
furnished with lichens, blazing ochre and rust.
The fields need shadow. You can hear them
clamor for it under the gurgle
of the draining washbasin. Do not resort
to professions of indifference.
I filled up my car with vegetables.
They are deliciously heavy and various,
and they rustle like a flock of birds.

> If a man has big ideas he is usually
> deemed insane; but I trust the
> community will not thrust the charge
> of insanity on me; but will allow me
> quietly to follow my own inspiration.
> —*Charles J. Guiteau*

I sat in a chair. No. It was a car,
it was a car with two flat tires
like the one Marilyn Monroe used to drive
in that movie I said I would write for her.

At any rate, I am made out of snow
as my brother Hank is, except he's made of silk,
silk with the slightest admixture of snow,
kind of the way you might see bursts of color
in a childhood dream of Leningrad.

In other poems, meanwhile, poets anatomized
the supple, yielding structure of reality,
as though they were Commissioner of Drought.
Their words were no different than mine.
The room filled slowly with silt. Deposit this
in a nearby mailbox whenever you can.
Oh here comes Hank, he wants to return

your notebook along with your other ear.
What I mean is, the airplane is surest to crash
just as the attendant serves a perfect martini
to the actress you adored since you were a girl.
I have a diagram which explains it all

but alas! Alan King got ahold of it,
and while underground it ate six Nacho Cheez Combos.
Now for six months of the year it bursts into flame
or demands to be combed, draped with fresh kelp,
and adorned with the sun's last light.

You see, all along I loved the festival.
My mother made my toes, she made them
disappear. Didn't you expect
such books to come back,
sometime in the middle of the night?
For once, the hard blue flowers all agreed.

Kuling

17

Grenada, Windward Islands, Aug. 1999

KULING
GRENADA, WINDWARD ISLANDS, AUG. 1999

CROWD

MATTHEW MONTEITH
UNTITLED

Matthew Monteith
Untitled

JANE HAMMOND
THE BREAD AND BUTTER MACHINE

OIL AND MIXED MEDIA ON WOOD PANEL
78¾" DIAMETER 6" DEEP

JANE HAMMOND
PART TIME IN THE LIBRARY

OIL ON CANVAS
74" X 98"

Christa Parravani
Tawasentha

On a train from Princeton    The brown seats are so flat    Sewn together    In steps of white thread    As though it had something to do with making things    With hands    Or with me (I have hands)    *Or* is gold in France    In college logic class    It means something else: *There is something else*    Deciding between various *versuses*    Joining the sentence on the left    With the sentence on the right    Making me chew a choose    The word holding two pieces    Like an antique button    A mark of division    Forming my clothes

My philosophy degree    Even explained this train    And the train to New York I missed last night    Even though I missed it    I miss it    You are on a train or you are not on a train    All the time    Even before I thought to mind    And had to sleep on a blue mat On someone's dorm room floor another night    Last night    Even though someone had broken my heart    And I wanted to go home    And binge eat    Everything on this train has a shape    Round up square sad

So many poems about transportation    And I figure    The figuring goes    I figure while I go    That has something to do with having    To be here on earth    And not being able to find enough    Ways to move    So saying to the stuckness    *Don't temper me    Don't temper me*

# Laure-Anne Bosselaar

## FOLLEN STREET

        I do it each time we move, did it
again to our new house in this shut
Cambridge street:

        press my forehead and palms
to the door, ask *Forgive me* before
I bring in my mess: relics,

        hopes, insomnia, clocks.
Then, while the one I love carefully
prints our names on the mailbox,

        I chase vacancy away with broom
and books, hang the paintings—
those fake windows I need

        to comfort me from what I keep
seeing through lucid ones: the same skies,
traffic, neurasthenic dogs and always,

        everywhere, the old widow
or widower trying to walk evenly and be
dapper: the woman

        with dust on her nice little hat
and too much blush;  the man in his brown
shoes and gray pants, an inch

too short: it gets me each time
that whole inch missing. And oh,
what they carry:

his briefcase flat, flagrantly
useless, but something to hold onto—
her bag clasped around

"just-in-cases" she never leaves
without: so much like what I bring
to this house—things, things

to hold onto in case night
freezes the shutters shut and only
my name remains on the mailbox.

# Rafael Campo

## Cuban Canticle No. 6
## Lucy, I'm Home!

26

Believe me when I tell you that I know
the sense of promise in that accent's roar—
the drama of arrival!—how intent
it is on its accomplishments, its spent
yet somehow infinite, simpatico,
American resolve: he's through the door,

his wife is beautiful, his eldest son
is watching satiny gray re-runs, all
the day's humiliations gone. I know
it's not that funny when, in the bright glow
of our nuclear-combustible
not quite perfect family, he begins

to talk about his dreams of something better.
I know he wants the best for me, but I
pretend I'm little Ricky and my mother
(she's zany, irresponsible, *alive*)
is telling some kind of terrible lie
that the whole world cannot help but forgive.

# Shanna Compton
## GRITTY, TOUGH-MINDED CAPER

The armored car man rides the train.
He wishes someone would approach him
and propose a grand heist,

like in the movies. All this sameness.
His feet are small, and he wears loafers
with goldtone embellishments.

Sometimes a uniform requires
these little indignities: A short-sleeve shirt and tie.
Perhaps this fuels his love of glamour.

The train stops.
Two moon-faced women board the car.
He whispers to them, *Let me hear your plan.*

# Michael Costello
## A Series

28

talent may be seen in his brilliant repetition…"
When flowers are ready, they change—
Why not take yourself as a subject, so that everything you do represents yourself?
Between differ and different is difference.
The cow makes
and remakes itself

as wallpaper again and again. Moment to moment *Mao* is like himself
and "questions of an artistic variety arise—regarding repetition
and appropriation"—everything Marilyn makes
is taken from her. The *flowers* change:
autonomous, remade, composing each petal is different
and the same, "there's nothing

behind it." Mao complains about something/everything/anything/nothing
Where? Everywhere. *Marilyn* is around herself.
But between *Green Marilyn* and another *Mint Marilyn* the difference
"…fought to show us there is no repetition…"
make changes
by burning out unwanted areas. Order makes

itself, orders itself to make
a straight line: before, during, after. Nothing,
is the thing to think of. Make no changes—
other than those of scale/medium/and installation—(to be as beautiful as) itself

"at times it is difficult to distinguish art from its repetition."
"These are flowers, and these are *flowers*." What's the difference?

Now is the difference.
Do a *Blue Electric Chair* and *Red Race Riot* make
for a *Lavender Disaster*? Time and repetition
are the central motifs in which nothing
is absolute, except itself,
and the *Silver Marlon* above it which does not change

the Brillo Box, but the *Brillo Box* is changed
and the amount found between beginning and end is the difference.
More and less the *Self-Portrait* becomes itself,
but why make
it? Make it (nothing no thing), it will be nothing
but *flowers cows Maos Marilyns* and their repetitions

Repetition changes
nothing—difference
makes itself.

# Lynn Crosbie
## ROACH FRENCH FRIES

I was given this diary by my friend Michael in Vancouver in the summer of 1999. It is a spiral bound paper notebook. On its cover is a red and yellow carton of golden, ketchup-dappled french fries against a pale blue background.

The carton says FRENCH FRIES. Above these words, someone has pasted this large black sticker: ROACH.

I was staying in Vancouver a few days before leaving to visit a friend in the Saanich Peninsula. I had packed a number of gourmet items—strawberries soaked in brandy; dwarf carrots pickled in vinegar. Michael and I drove around in his Ford Tempo a lot, listening to "She's a Rainbow," with the windows rolled down.

On Robson Street I bought a short story written by a homeless kid. Two pages of foolscap, the story involved a Viking named William, who "had some blondish facial hair which could easily grow into a flowing beard."

Michael gave me the diary, and showed me his rock garden. Turning over the earth, he had discovered pieces of bone china with disparate patterns: cabbage roses, vines, interlocking gold and silver teeth.

I saw a pod of Orcas surface by the ferry; in Sidney, ducklings appeared in the creek. I met a black cat named Lily. My friend was desperately ill.

I read the diary while I was there.

I have not been able to locate the owner of *Roach French Fries*. I tried the two telephone numbers inside. Calvin + Steve (9301 Avendale Rd., in Redmond) and "Open Distance Learning." The first has been disconnected; the second is an automated student services line.

I do not know the writer's name. She is a high school student, who knows 19 gymnastic moves including "Angel, Angel Mermaid," "Wappidy up to Standing," "Toothpick Move," "Bird's Nest on Ropes" and "Becky Stag."

Her poetry is fairly disquieting though I think not uncommon at this age: *The loveliness I once found painted/In a flower has been erased &/The contagouse smile held in a childs/Eye has been terminated by vaccination.*

She has made the following, in my opinion, trenchant observations:

Her friend Nuala should stop laughing that way. It's fake and frankly unsettling.

Lisa and Dido are only interested in clothes and looking cool.

Matthew has stopped calling altogether. What's wrong with him?

Although there is not much that she wants from life, she has made three wishes:

    —"I wish I had a smile that would put people at ease & make them happy."
    —"I wish people loved me for who I am."
    —"I wish new good 100% friends who loved me would find me."

I find myself close to loving the writer I now call "Debbie" 100% and I feel at ease, happy about this.

Debbie feels her mother is "bitchy & anal-retentive," that only she can see what she's really like:

Debbie, I felt this too.

I am looking through my 1977 diary, burgundy leather with an incomprehensible Russian insignia.

At 14 I wrote poetry:

> *Grasp the liquid eyeball*
> *melt the purple shine*
> *squeeze the black dot*
> *and poke the white sea.*
> *Scream when you see the madness*
> *and withdraw in horror…*

and referred to my mother with very little civility, or manners.

You are sitting in a restaurant, writing and drawing cross-hatched pictures of men and women falling; a tree of faces; a burning hand. There are two aquaintances beside you who do not say hello, *As if you care.*

I drew and passed around pictures of old men with tree-sized erections; a woman lifting her skirt, revealing a man buried inside, legs kicking. I was thrown out of class often for similar transgressions, *As if I cared.*

You are wondering if insane people can read your thoughts; if you could read other people's thoughts, what would that be like?

It would be something like this: invasive and obscene.

I am thinking about you now, after your diary leaves off. Years passing, and still wanting the same things, love and ease; still wondering why people hurt you; a little lonely, and defiant:

*I wonder if I'm going to become some minimum wage shittily paid blue collar worker or will I make it. Kill me now just do it.*

You call these fears, what makes you "nervose," "this teendom thing":
Debbie, nothing changes.

I visited Vancouver again this Spring—six years after my first trip to read poetry at a little club with a bongo-player. I fell in love there too, in a way.

There was something about the cherry blossoms falling so sweetly, and slowly, time seemed like this to me then, suspended and ripe.

At the time I was working through a roll of Valium, feeling as high as you get sometimes Debbie ("I saw Jesus/and an Angel in a burst of life"), and filled with half-baked heartache:

"Brians leaving for Chilli soon & if he doesn't call before he leaves, I'll cry."

When I returned, I called him and he never called back. I cried and began throwing things.

Donna, an old friend of mine, moved from Toronto to Vancouver, and lived on Thurlow Street—she had become a lawyer, and enjoyed shopping. I visited her and told her he never called.

"I hate life & I think life hates me."

My lawyer friend was infuriated by my inability to see clearly. He doesn't care about you, she said. She laughed in a fake, unsettling way.

I'm afraid that's not possible, I told her. I went out alone and bought Chinese lottery tickets, scratched them under a tree. The blossoms fell, tumbling like paradise.

Something that you wrote, in a poem called "On the Streets, Love," reminds me. That cities contain your feelings, shake and whirl them through the air, love, and hate—

Debbie, I was saying that, recently, I visited Vancouver again.

"There's no Princes, so I'll save myself."

The odourless cherry trees looked like plastic kitsch; my friend was not able to come to the phone.

I saw an old acquaintance panhandling for junk in Gastown, and he was the nicest person I met.

Riding with Michael in the Ford Tempo, we listened to Keith Richard's country songs, cruel complaints.

Donna and I went shopping and she gave me a dragon fruit. I wrote a poem about it later that I never finished, which was all idea and no execution—

> The Dragon Fruit
>
> The deep rose oval, its flesh furled like crimson flags
> Sat on the night table at the Sylvia Hotel
> For three days, simmering.
>
> I had not travelled with a knife, defenseless
> The dragon fruit
> Nestled with unanswered messages,
>
> A pink dress in yellow tissue paper, glasses
> Filled with Sapphire gin and ice.
>
> The gulls flew straight at the window,
> Crows and doves.

"I've got some awesome ideas," you wrote.

The fruit was supposed to be a metaphor for Donna, for the fight we would have, where I walked away, carrying four suitcases up the high streets and moving farther from the ocean, the mountains veiled in storm clouds.

The gulls and so on represent a new interest in birds, in taking their pictures.

At your age I would play Lynyrd Skynyrd and close my eyes: *I'm as free as a bird, man—*

Incidentally, one of your rap songs mentions "the fowls of violation."

Donna and I are no longer speaking. Lily was killed by a car; my friend died. I now regard Vancouver to be an ugly city, without allure.

"I grew a painful soul"

I wondered in my diary what it would be like, at this age, not knowing how I would feel, moving against the wind on steep inclines,

immersing pain in anger, pain, like a roach in a box of french fries—you understand this awful paradox:

"To be loved and to love. That is the secret. I've got half of it down."

I've got half of it down.

# Connie Deanovich

## ADDICTION TO HITCHCOCK, TAKE SEVEN

She was trapped
her desires drew strings through her heart

Besides aspirin
Hope was taking two movies daily

*Strangers on a Train* gulped down with
careful-what-you-wish-for water

The hands of Bruno the stranger
become strangler's hands when you add the *L*

*L* for liquor and lunatic
and luck

Never before had Hope
seen a Hitchcock in the mountains

The forest out the window
like a rusty minefield

The sharp hills and jagged trees
shutting out the world—dank, dangerous, and January

CROWD Magazine
119 North 11th Street 1A
Brooklyn, NY 11211

# I MUST BE PART OF THE CROWD

I LOVE CROWD SO MUCH I'D GIVE YOU A MILLION DOLLARS IF I HAD IT. IN FACT, I'D GIVE YOU TWO MILLION DOLLARS. I'D GIVE YOU MY GOOD SHOES AND THAT NEW SUEDE JACKET. I'D GIVE YOU MY LITTLE SISTER. I'D GIVE YOU MY LAPTOP IF I KNEW IT MEANT YOU WOULD KEEP PUBLISHING THIS WONDEROUS THING YOU CALL A MAGAZINE.

## BUT INSTEAD, I'LL SEND YOU 20 DOLLARS AND I'LL GET A ONE YEAR SUBSCRIPTION

$20 a year (two issues). Single-copy price is $12.
Please make checks payable to CROWD Magazine,
119 North 11th Street 1A, Brooklyn, NY 11211

info@crowdmagazine.com

When imagination is dangerous
it puts its hands around a woman's throat

And has ideas for harnessing the "life force"
for smelling the flowers on Mars

The imagination unbalanced
is so much trouble

Its cleverness floats through an angry tunnel
its moxie gets socked in the jaw

Strangling is the best action cinematically
because it's so silent

And Hitchcock rewards it
over and over

Lobster claws on a necktie
mother manicuring the killer as if he's a pharaoh

What's wrong is the picture spun by the merry-go-round
when it's out of control

Hero and villain fighting
like the wishes of the heart

The exposed throat is so refreshingly blunt
it says "here is where you kill me"

It says "here is the instrument for voice,
destruction, salvation"

Hope stirs her Bloody Mary
then takes a good hard swallow

Pepper and tomato and vodka
stinging her lips like the lights of a slideshow

# Connie Deanovich
## LITTLE GOTHIC PICTURE

Talked so much today

I want to cut off my tongue

and put it in a tiny coffin

# Geoffrey DeTrani

## EVOLUTION REDRESSED

40

It's in the nature of evolution
To trade beforeishness for afterhood

A nostalgia projected out,
A thin imaginary axis
Fortified with the supple shape
Mirrors and glinting glass

It's in the nature of evolution
To speak your native language

Softly, with proper inflection
Compressing the gesture of effect
With the pathos of cause
From a spot deep in the voice

Speech in a crude pidgin
Mouthed by house builders,
Gesturing masons
Bricked path to the pacifry
Ditch, drain, cultivation pit
Prior, prior, now

Home to petite pacifiers
A cenotaph, a pacific ocean
Tucked well under floor boards

sweet slow take off
was the original intent

only a trick line connected
this ecstatic body to
that able means

august, liquefied

fits and starts in natural
order. eyeshots like
billy clubs flexed
eyes out-selfed with
concave thresholds bending
august freely

drag it out
to the melting pond
with cooling rods the
post emptive
sentimentalizers
cataloging the difference from
sweet slow take off

# Geoffrey DeTrani
## MNEMONIC DEVICE

42

stop punching holes in that
rosetta stone
useful for tricking Mnemosyne
useful for grabbing souvenirs from a
muted future

I stopped growing penicillin on the
livingroom floor
stopped humping coal for heat

you came in holding the
common device
which raft floats best?
you are the next door neighbor
talk about the blessings of family life
birthday candles and mouthfuls because
it would be ruinous to be ahistorical

# Trane Devore
## Our Age

Old, in the dark,
we cry out strange and strangely
while the women inside
trail the doorways with white gauze—

we examine, like in hospitals,
our skin—its creases and tears,
where it dries or peels its waft off,
(taken to becoming dust grains).

In time, a fine coagulate
appears along the road like snow:

here we find ourselves by tea-leaves—
our disintegration laps the days,
our steeping detritus reveals the dark meaning
of inveterate whorls.

# Ray DiPalma
## SLEEPING IN THE NETS

44

Negligent, I heard it
before anything else
could be clearly defined

*Before* being
a time when
there was no necessity

The evidence blurred
by imagined elaborations
news, weather, and plenty of music

An over-extended horizontal arrow
turned vertical—a hard right enclosing
the moderations of desire and decay

Scene: You show up unexpectedly
and do not act like yourself.

On a crowded summer street we encounter
carnival performers, barbershop crooners,
a walking catfish with the tops
of a turnip hanging from its mouth.

A man in a candy-stripe suit announces
it is now possible to swim from Chicago
to New York in an hour and a half.
You are seventy-two and decide to try it.

Crowds line the walls and cheer as we go by.
We rise from the canal completely dry,
and, face forward, you move through the crowd
with the confidence of a ghost.

I follow behind obediently,
asking questions you do not answer:
"Where have you been?"
"Why can't you stay longer?"

Each time we meet like this
I tell myself a tale born
of my own half-baked beliefs.
Perhaps death is just life in reverse.

Perhaps you are now a girl
swimming in the Adriatic
and do not speak to me
because we are no longer acquainted.

my mother says that in third grade I looked so mature that another parent mistook me for a teacher on the first day of school though that can't be true    I must have been only four feet tall at the most    I remember my girlish outfits    ankle socks and a green felt dress I loved so much that the girls made fun of me for wearing it over and over    I remember Becky Bilieu saying *what's the matter you poor or something*    I didn't really know what she meant but my mother was in the hospital again so I thought maybe poor meant lacking a mother    *we're going to get her* I heard Becky say to a group of girls that looking back now were poorer than I was and I hated that to get her looked like the word *together* with spaces inserted    *to get her* didn't sound like *together* when you put it together because of the *th*    whenever Becky pronounced a word with *th* dots of spit would collect in the corners of her mouth    I wasn't together with my mother because something was wrong with her that was hard for my father to talk about    sometimes I was glad that my mother was gone to get her life back together in a hospital where no kids were running around making noise and that's probably why I looked old enough in third grade to be a miniature teacher    I knew the importance of being mature and responsible and organized and quiet    I didn't tell my father about Becky and the poor girls who circled me on the girl's side of the playground and said *we're going to get you real bad* I just told him I split my lip when I fell down I just told him I hated the green dress I'd loved the day before

when my husband was little his mother told him *never feel inferior my darling you are a Carbó* maybe she told him that because she believed it or because he was adopted and Filipino and although she was white she knew a thing or two about self-esteem and race

my mother never said anything about our last name or what it meant though for years I translated it from the French to *of the valley* which explained my overuse of the word *like* but then a few weeks ago I met a French scholar at a party who said *ah Duhamel    of the hamlet   your people originally must have been from a small village* and I felt clueless like the valley girl I had identified with all those years before she became a stock character of sit-coms and stand-up

*give me some Carbó* I tell my husband when it's cold and I want him to come to bed    sometimes I forget the accent over the o and he becomes Carbo like a carbohydrate instead of the more regal iamb his last name is

I remember Bubba at the chalkboard in seventh grade an unyielding algebra problem before him and mean Mrs. Martin hoping to reduce him to tears *come on this is an easy one* Mrs. Martin said *anyone can do it whether you're an Einstein or a Duhamel* and I never understood why she said that    I was one of her best students    I assumed she meant Duhamels and Einsteins were polar opposites

———————

anyway that's what I wrote on the N train from Astoria Boulevard to Lexington Avenue where I changed for the 6 because I have to get to Grand Central to catch a Metro North train to Philipse Manor where I teach a class    when I was trying to write on the N a kid sitting next to me kept saying over and over *get the crayons* to his mother who said she wouldn't get them until he said *please get the crayons    get the crayons* the kid said like a rap song the same words in different intonations    louder then softer    whiny then menacing    I wanted to say *that's enough now stop* it in a gruff mother voice    the kid's own mother was zoned out as though the subway's Radio City poster was a TV as though all those Rockette legs would begin dancing at any moment    now on the 6 train a smaller child is crying half coughing    his mother has put plastic over his stroller since it's so cold out and the plastic has condensation on it like a shower curtain    I first saw the Rockettes on Ed Sullivan    a camera shot looking down from the ceiling of all the dancers making a circle shape lying on the floor head to head their legs zigzagging like opening and closing petals

———————

maybe because of all the self help books I've read    maybe because of therapy    I always have the urge to sum things up in writing    to end with some big closure instead of an image    now on Metro North I'm tempted to say that I became a little wife to my father when my mother was away and that's why I looked like a teacher in third grade instead of a kid but actually I remember my dad being the daddy    making blushing bunnies grilled cheese sandwiches with tomato slices    or opening a can of corned beef hash at both ends and sliding out the pinkish gray tube of meat in one piece    potato bits the size of confetti    he'd slice it to make corned beef patties he'd fry one with an egg on top for him    I didn't feel like a third grade wife    I wish I knew how to meditate then maybe I'd have access to more memories

my friend who's using Reiki to heal is writing her life story    virtually every memory she can remember in more or less chronological order    she's been writing for two months now and she's only up to when she was five    she's remembering all these poignant details her parents having long lunches while she and her brother played in the grass on the other side of a sliding glass door    I can't tell you why in hindsight this image is so poignant because that's her story    a story she's trying to make sense of but believe me very sad and horrible things are about to happen with the glass and the mother    I used to be interested in self healing as well    I used to try to write affirmations in the eighties but my mind always started to wander and I could never stick to the affirmation at hand    I remember trying to write *I am rich and thin*    that was my affirmation    but I'd never be able to write it more than three times in a row without getting other ideas

I am thin and rich
I eat rich foods    I have a thin wallet
I eat the rich who are not as rich as I am
I have thin skin and a rich husband
I have rich skin and a thin husband
I am rich when it comes to thinness
I wear a thin dress    but it doesn't mean I'm thin
I wear a rich dessert on my chin
I have a thin chin and a rich waist
the rich waste food    that's why they're thin
the thin waste everything    the thin waste away
the rich milk chocolate taste of the rich

the rich milk chocolate taste of the thin
a thin mint is not rich
the rich have a mint    that's why they're rich
the thin are as thin as lines in a coloring book
I'm rich and a person of one color or another
I am thin and a rich dark blue
even the rich are sometimes blue
even the thin are sometimes green with envy
I envy the rich    especially the rich who are thin
envy is a thin tinny emotion rich with complications
but not according to that book I read
the author says it's simple to be rich and thin
so that's what I am

---

on the way home from my class the Metro North is so different    during peak hours it's filled with business people returning to their Westchester homes but now it's mostly college kids and people who look like domestic help  like they may have spent the whole day cleaning or taking care of someone else's children    I wonder about my friend who's writing down her whole life what strange click will occur the day she finishes her story and writes something like so *I guess that takes me to this very moment now*    she'll be purged    a China white plate    a clean silver-framed window    it will be a little death just like birth is a little death since birth means a separation

---

it seems to me my friend will never remember everything    even as she puts down her pen on that final day she might remember a loose button on the coat she wore in ninth grade    that the name of the hill leading to her school was Ascension Street    that those gray cobblestones were slippery in winter    how she took baby-steps just like in One Two Three Red Light terrified of falling while her classmates zipped by    sliding on purpose sitting on improvised sleds    the sides torn off cardboard boxes    while she stood frozen both cold and still    clutching the cement indentations that  separated the brick on the building which must have been a factory because there were slabs of green wood over the windows and billowing smoke coming out of what looked to her like a clothes dryer vent

whether that's my memory or my friend's doesn't matter    what is important says my friend's healer are the same small details    or else somebody tells you something about your past that makes you see it in a whole new way    my sister recently told me for the first time that when I was hit by a car    bumped really    with only a few bruises    she walked home and said to my mother *Denise is dead*    someday someone will say that sentence and mean me and it will be true but then I was only six with at least 31 more years to live    those 31 years which bring me to this very moment    my sister telling me this made me feel so bad for my mother who ran red lights to get to the hospital    and even though all these years I thought she hated me the way my sister tells this story it is as though my mother couldn't bear the thought  of me being dead    I'd gotten into the car with my father and the teenaged driver who hit me which would never happen now because of law suits    *were you happy I was dead* I asked my sister who said when she was five she thought anyone hit by something as big as a car had to die    she said she was neither happy nor sad that death was a neutral concept to her back then

I remember the bracelet a neighbor gave me as a get-well present    a thick gold band with a huge blue flower popping out    I recently found it again in a box of my childhood stuff and it was a piece of junk    sort of a cheap filigree metal that's all rusted by now    the blue flower was the same metal    the petals popping out with their sharp dangerous edges it's hard to believe my mother let me wear the bracelet to school since it was at least an inch wide and clearly a bracelet for adults but I do remember wearing it    sort of showing off    even pretending it was real gold    a gift from the doctor in the emergency room    when my sister was a senior in high school she was hit by a car and wound up in a coma and I remember that for one horrible second I thought that maybe if she died my then-boyfriend would at least be nicer to me which is the reason I wouldn't have blamed my sister for wishing me dead at five so that she could have her own room and double the toys    my friend Lisa was also hit by a car when she was six when she was on her way to school and a car swerved out of control and up on the sidewalk knocking over a few garbage cans and then her    and because of that moment she was in a body cast for years and lost her spleen    my friend Maureen almost died when she was six from spinal meningitis    Maureen and Lisa and I all became writers everyone on this train has a story    the young woman tapping her thumb on her bright yellow Sony walkman    the older man in dirty work boots falling asleep with his mouth open and what would it be like if the conductor said over the speaker *this train is not stopping at Grand Central tonight everyone take out a sheet of paper* and because his voice sounded like God's we all obeyed    what if all we passengers started writing everything we could remember in chronological order all the way down the Hudson all the way through the American South all the way through South American down to Antarctica    where would we wind up

# MK Francisco
## Tuy Ly

*Leader of the anti-French resistance in 1884 under Than Thi*

from the last respite. thimbles of blood. and the authorized sale of opium. cloud-fish crowned. to balance them off each other. abandoned the use of chinese characters. chinese irregulars like black flags. obtuse, frisson, theorem, parallax. he triple oiled his hair. the malarial orchestra reticent. the old language repeating only stone, tree. dragon, mountain. hanging over fire or water. peeled chickens. lucent poisson. similarly a steady drip of missionaries. not pessimisms nor sorcery. *to go too far is as bad as not to go far enough.*

# Kristen Hanlon

## THE WORD THEY CALL WATER KEEPS RISING

54

Errands practiced in solitude.

Then a ragged deliverance:
attempted dialogue with a stranger
becomes "give us a kiss!"

Mutiny complete,
birds sleep.

Bliss, that mirage—

Is it human to be this hungry,
is my envoy an answer
or question?

Harrison Haynes
Gloaming No. 2

Watercolor on Paper
11" x 15"

JOE BRAINARD & RON PADGETT
UNTITLED

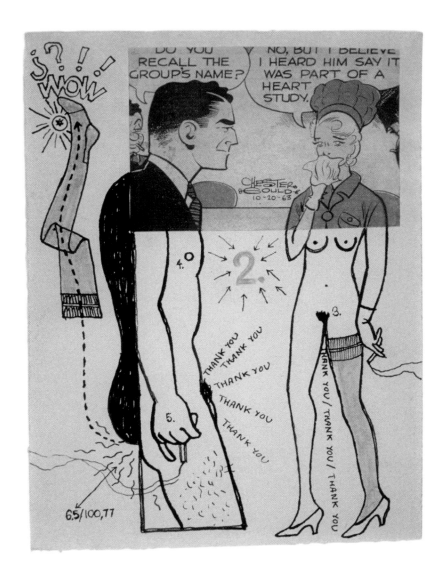

JOE BRAINARD & RON PADGETT
UNTITLED

JOE BRAINARD & RON PADGETT
UNTITLED

JOE BRAINARD & RON PADGETT
UNTITLED

HARRISON HAYNES
WILDWOOD FLOWER

ACRYLIC ON PAPER
26¾" x 30"

Me—who am as a nerve o'er which do creep
The else unfelt oppressions of this earth.
    *—Shelley*

*Completely normal*, he wrote, *for man years completely normal*, then he took out *man* and put in *many*.

———————

Maybe he had just spent too long working the nerves. Nerve fibers once had a reputation as aphrodisiacs, and were fashioned into amulets for daily wear, from simple rings and bracelets to elaborate knit codpieces. In the town where George grew up locals believed to this day that a walk in the nerve fields made women ovulate and a handful of freshly cut nerve fibers under the pillow brought true dreams of love. A nap in the fields had more lasting consequences: George's town, like every small town in the Great Plains, had one or two children known as *nervous*. They were said to be the offspring of the plains themselves, and their mothers were blamed for nothing more damning than carelessness. Sceptical outsiders might take note of the many flattened patches in the fields near town, and the well-trodden paths that lead to them.

Tender, susceptible fields! A careless boot sent a wave of consternation seven miles. A gunshot made the plains flinch to their last hummock. But at night, when lovers lay in congress in the fields, the pale strands flexed contentedly against the black sky. Concentric rings spread from their several centers and collided in elaborate interference patterns that made the whole plains hum a particular note. In the village they heard the note. They recognized it, they smiled, they fell back asleep. Or they worked out the harmony on their creaking beds. George used to lie awake, listening.

———————

*Completely normal*, wrote George, though he remembered going to his mother and saying, "Mom, am I nervous?"

"No, of course not, what put that idea into your sick little head?" Mom had said, and what George remembered was that he was disappointed. So, a desire to be special, even then.

*Completely normal*, wrote George, then selected the passage and rendered it in bold, as if to spite his own memory.

---

Cut nerves left lying on threshing floors drift and roll and wind up all lined up with the earth's magnetic field, like iron filings swayed by a magnet in a classroom experiment. (Bring a smaller magnet into the barn and watch them try to follow it!) But there are places where the magnetic field of the earth is disorganized, the ley lines tangled. Compass needles wag; carrier pigeons lose their way.

It so happened that a big nerve supplier built a warehouse in one of these places, and that George worked there. Big signs were posted all over the building: Clean Up After Yourselves. All Nerves Must Be Bundled. And simply, Sweep. The workers were meticulous, by and large. All the same it was bound to happen: a nerve slipped out of a bundle, slithered under a pallet, went unnoticed. In a few days, another one got away. After a while there were four, five, twenty-five scattered here and there around the warehouse: under tables, in cracks in the floor, snagged on splinters in the door frame.

Slowly, slowly, they were drawn together. Some moved like inchworms, humping up. Some like sidewinders. Some just slithered. They amassed: a pale, luminous pile in what moonlight found its way through the dusty windows.

Nerve fibers have a curious property. They organize themselves. They twine, knot, braid, lace, plait, mesh, splice. Some stringent ancient script takes over.

By midnight, a thick braid lay shining on the ground. (At home, George was sleeping quietly for the last time in his life.) Over the ensuing hours, more strands knotted themselves to it. They formed nosegays, posies, faggots. Sheafs and bales. (George slept on.) They twisted, coiled, fretted themselves together. (George woke up, took a hard-boiled egg out of the fridge, baggied it, shook some salt into the bag, set out early for work.)

A forked figure stood, took a bite of the apple.

George's key turned in the lock.

---

These spontaneous assemblages of sensibility are not just admired by aestheticians and teenaged girls. One minute you're a man of business, the next you're writing sonnets to a squiggle of sore pasta, and your career can go to hell for all you care.

The warehouse supplied nerve fibers to top designers. George handled the overseas clients. He was a burly, well-spoken man, with clean, filed fingernails. Nobody would have pegged him for the sort to ditch the wife and kids (not yet an actual wife and kids, but a prospective wife and kids, real enough that he could almost see their tiny resentful faces as they waved goodbye) and go in for pain and sequins. Nobody including him. But there he was, in love with a length of forked lightning.

How long was that going to last? But it changed everything. Afterwards, he found that he remembered his past differently. Isolated incidents suddenly strung themselves together into an argument, a prediction. Innocent objects started to phosphoresce. A child's Rainy Day Fun Book metamorphosed into a grimoire.

――――――――――

"Tie a Turk's Head in a hank of nerves—four fibers will do. Give the nerves a turn to make a neck. Reserve two fibers for the arms. Twist the remaining two together to make the body of your nerve man or lady. When half of their length is still remaining, separate them to form the legs. Give them a little loop at the end so the dolls have feet to stand on. Keep your eye on them while you fashion their outfits—don't let them get away!

"Here are some easy outfits you can make. Cut a dress out of plain paper. Tape the nerve lady to the back side. You may want to draw a pocket or an apron on the dress. Your nerve gentleman does not need much clothing, but perhaps you will want to give him a natty bow tie! Cut it out of plain paper and give it a gay pattern with your crayons. How about polka dots? Or stripes? Now your nerve gentleman is ready to step out with the lady of the house.

"Maybe you would like to give your nerve man and lady a shoe-box house to live in. Glue a piece of patterned paper on the floor to make a rug. You can cut out miniature pictures for the walls, or draw windows for them to look out of. Chairs can be made out of corks and nails, see page 23. Do they like to watch TV? Draw a scene from your favorite TV program on the front of a box, and add some dials. Use your imagination!

"When you're finished playing, just put on the lid to keep them safe and sound until next time."

――――――――――

"It was cruel," George told his therapist. "But children are cruel, aren't they? Not evil, but nonchalant about pain. I was interested in salting slugs, swatting flies. Of course the general opinion at the time was that the nerve dolls didn't suffer because they weren't really alive to begin with. Frog legs kick in the lab with no frog attached to them, you know. Chickens gad about without their heads.

"They weren't the best-looking dolls. No more than stick figures. Their paper-doll dresses hung crooked, and exposed their backsides whenever they turned around. How I laughed!

"Now I regret the bow ties and aprons. What an impertinence. The poor things were in agony. They were just alive enough to feel pain. A knot of appetite and no insulation. An erect twinge, a stitch on tip-toe.

"They waltzed, after a fashion, holding each other up so as little of them as possible touched the ground. Then they fizzed, smoked, fell over and 'died.' 'Boo hoo!' I cried, 'Boo hoo!' and held little funerals. That was my favorite part."

---

Not that pain is the worst thing in the universe. Interesting things happen when you adopt pain for your own. This thing you were prepared to spend your life flinching from is suddenly just another piece of information.

George began to feel that his own comfort was an affront. Sitting on the toilet, he squeezed the rolls of fat around his middle, cupped his breasts, measuring. Somewhere inside George was another George: spiderlike, avid, flexile. Like grammar, but physical. George wanted to make himself into this other George so that he would be more like his lover and by being like him, possess him again. So he ate less and less and during lunch at the warehouse he picked up some fibers and played cat's cradle with himself. When he could not help himself but eat, when it was someone's birthday and everyone sang and there were cupcakes with candles on them, he learned how to make himself vomit up the sweet sludge before it stuck.

---

Cat's cradle used to be a game for priests and princes. It retains a whiff of the sacred. You are playing a game with string, then you are in the milieu of the miraculous.

Every once in a while, through luck or incredible skill, a figure is actually perfect. An instant is long enough: the cat's cradle kindles. Flames run along the fibers. A glyph of fire stands in the air. It goes out a second later; all that's left is a blue smoke, a weird smell, a fading cicatrix on your retina. Your hands fall away.

———————————

"Everything perfect burns itself up," George told his therapist. "A perfect thing does not have to hang around, it has satisfied all the requirements of existing. That's what Deja says. Or maybe a perfect thing can't hang around, because perfection has no place in our world, which is a world of approximates. Existence is approximation; we are because of a kind of blurring of the material world. All attempts at perfection are destructive, therefore."

"Want to talk about this diet you're on?" said his therapist.

———————————

French designer Deja, one of George's best customers, had made the front page news world-wide when his electric dresses burst into flames on the runway and disappeared in a puff of smoke, leaving two of his models naked and innocent of body hair.

"Well," shrugged Deja in newsprint, "it simply means I achieved a perfect form. Perfection cannot last." One model later revealed that she had not had any body hair to begin with. This had not stopped Deja, next spring, from bringing out a triumphant new line of depilatory dresses for ladies, depilatory culottes and tunics pour l'homme. "All have sold sensationally in Europe, but American customs officials have refused to allow them in the country. Yes they are dangerous—so is l'amour, which recognizes no boundaries!"

George read the article to his therapist. "As yet, France is the only country where you may attend the opera with your head in flames, but American scene-makers were seen passing a petition at the Paris and Milan shows, so we may see a relaxation of the policy yet.

"Buyers have conveyed to Deja their customers' requests for depilatory panties that can be worn to work. 'Our customers love the idea of depilatory clothes, but are afraid to go to the office in a dress that may go poof,' they say. 'Many of our customers are successful women in high-paying jobs and must maintain a professional demeanor,' they insist. 'Unfortunately naked says unprofessional to these women.' So far Deja is resisting the pressure, though underlings have dropped hints that he may soften his stance in time for fall. We spoke to him in his Paris atelier.

"'Beauty must be convulsive or not at all, isn't it?' he says. 'I give the people something to look at, like it or not.'

"There was a flash of light and his pants disappeared. We saw what he meant."

———————

"Boys don't do this," thought George, his soft breasts shrinking, parallel horizontal creases appearing in his stomach, a strange side effect of weight loss, his ribs appearing, knuckles appearing. "This is what girls do," then he was filled with pity for girls, and admiration for their love of will over appetite.

George was no longer looking very much like himself, hair dry and wispy, bruises on his arms, George with a broken blood vessel in his right eye from puking too hard, eye flooded with cardinal red, the whites not white, closing in on the pupil, which stayed blue, however. Lapis and ruby. He tried to keep his eyes lowered till this condition passed, so as not to flash his single soiled petal, his damned spot. He was appalled but slightly thrilled by this disfiguring mark. He celebrated by burning off all his pubic hair with one of Deja's new samples. He was purifying.

———————

A guitar can be strung with nerve fibers. It is difficult to play, since nerves stretch: every note bends. The sound is unearthly, instantly recognizable, and not to everyone's taste. It enjoyed a brief vogue in psychedelic music, then reestablished itself as a solo instrument, where problems of tuning are less evident. Very few modern pieces have been written for the nerve guitar, since the plaintive traditional melodies are so rich in variations and so difficult to master that most guitarists spend their lives learning to play them, and prize nuanced performance over an original tune. (Chanter Ramos, who in the seventies used to strap on a nerve guitar to head his fifteen-member band of multi-culti artistes, was a figure of fun to these musicians.) On stormy or sexy nights, when the plains hum, you can sometimes hear a solitary nerve guitarist start up a descant over the drone. There is no more piercing or desolate sound.

George had sneered at this music when he was a kid. Now it was the only true and necessary music for him. He listened to it on headphones while he worked.

"They call them 'nervous systems.' Baloney. They're people," George told his therapist." The so-called *system* I fell in love with had more personality than I do. He loved tin lunchboxes, exotic weapons, tiny sugary cakes. He had delicacy and whimsy, but also the thirst for knowledge. Think Audrey Hepburn as Marie Curie: a pretty dress and a pocket full of radium.

"He was a kind of tuning fork. He vibrated with a perfect pain. I trued my pain to his and my pleasures fell into harmony as well. I had never felt so much, but it was nothing beside what he could feel; he was a perfect receiver. But you could see that for him, pleasure also hurt. There wasn't any difference, really, between pleasure and pain."

----

George got fired.

"It's not that you're not doing a good job, because you are. It's just that the other fellas find you... unnerving." The boss had a good laugh, then clapped George on the shoulder. "Sorry about that!" He composed himself. "We like you, George, and it's good sensitivity training for the guys to learn to work with someone with your condition, but frankly you get on their nerves and—sorry! Sorry! And output suffers. I've got to ask myself what's best for the corporate body as a whole. I'm thinking it'll be better for you too in the long run. You'll be able to put in for unemployment, take a little break, change of pace. It's gotta be good to get out of temptation's reach—right?"

As he left, he heard someone mutter, "Nervous Nellie!" An uneasy laugh rippled around the room. He put on his headphones.

----

"One minute, a bundle of nerves, the next, they're demanding Purcell, performance art, the times of their lives," George told his therapist. "Oh, it's so hard to watch them, swaying and longing. They want to be ballerinas. They want to marry Bluebeard, be tempted, and rub and rub at the bloodstain on their finger. They ask for frocks, opium, a ruby—just one!

"They look nothing like us. They look like a gardener's experiment run to seed, they look like macramé sculptures. But they appreciate us, none better. They want to try taxidermy. They say, I've got stigmata! They love Soutine, Ensor, tap dancing. They know how to live.

"They're not aliens. They are not animals. Give them a break! They are newborn, and terribly easy to hurt. Let them attempt the French horn, what harm can it do them? Give them typewriters. I'm seeing this now. I'm wishing I could have him back, start over. Ever read Frankenstein? I didn't give him the nurturing environment he needed. I was too, I have to use the word, unnerved."

"Why don't you go home for the holidays," his therapist suggested. "It's your birthday, too, isn't it; you're a December baby. You've got some free time now. Touch base with family. Consider letting them in on what you've been going through. It's a risk worth taking."

————————

"It's that time of year again, and here's your friendly fireman to deliver our annual safety tip: keep nerves away from bare bulbs and candles! Nerve tinsel is only safe for trees without Christmas lights. It looks pretty, but it's a real fire hazard. The same goes for garlands. Nerve wreaths are safe, but wear rubber gloves if you weave your own, and don't hang them within reach of the little ones.

"Let's keep one jingle bell from ringing this December: the fire bell!"

————————

"My word, that's a nice suit," said George's mother. "A bit flashy maybe. But it certainly has a nice hang. You must have lost weight. You look gaunt. Have some birthday cake. George! Take off your headphones while I'm talking to you."

————————

"I love you, wrecker of homes, ruination of family holidays," George wrote, "because you're a lightning rod, a perfect conductor for electricity and orchestras, a magnifying glass in the sun with a wisp of smoke sidling out from under it. You're a one-note solo that pierces our eardrums. You're a jungle gym heating up under the sun, branding our baby fat.

"I love you because flesh is stupid, like everything we build in imitation of the flesh: concrete blocks, sofas, airbags, all these hunks of dumb stuff that protect us. You're the cure for this sinus infection that stands in for a life, all the gluey textures of social intercourse and the bland obstructions. I'd carve off my own flesh in strips, leaving only the nerves, to spend one moment in pure apprehension. I want the skinny."

————————

"How could you, George. I've never heard anything so ridiculous. This is just a story you've cooked up to try me in my old age. You look terrible, you look sick, you've got some crazy ideas in your head, they're probably hallucinations from not eating. Here.

One slice is not going to hurt you, and I won't hear any more about this so-called love affair; you're just trying to shock me."

———————

"I know this is unreasonable, that only a fanatic can't forgive the pile-up of innocuous by-products of the life-well-lived. Matisse (the pure line, the untempered aquamarine) compared a painting to an armchair, and Dickens made people laugh. I know the guru on the mountaintop is just a cartoon. Real life is lived in the details, the plastic Teletubbies cups and the bottle-resealers that don't quite work. We drop dead cells by the billions and go racing on in a flurry of dandruff, we fill holes with empty Yoplait containers, there is no economy to our carrying on, nor should there be. I suspect that only the comfortable value pain. But I want a short arachnoid life of art and acrobatics and leave the curds and whey to others. I want a life like a squib: one sizzle and I'm out."

———————

"For me? It's not my birthday." She ripped the paper off. "Well. Now that's what I call a hat. Where did you get your sense of style? Certainly not from your father. When will I have any chance to wear something like this out here in the boondocks? It certainly is elegant, though—"

"Don't try it now, Mom. Mom! Don't—"

After they had extinguished the blaze, and Mom had settled her second-best wig on her head, pointedly allowing the once best to sizzle on in the kitchen sink, George went to the upstairs bathroom and rid himself of the cake, making no attempt to keep the noise down. Then he went out. He walked to the edge of town, grinding his teeth gently together, reflecting on how the freshly acid-washed enamel made this more of a rubbing than a sliding sensation, and subtly unpleasant. He crossed the drainage ditch, stepping onto what looked like a solid bank, and his right shoe filled with icy water. The cold began to wick up his wool sock. Right, notice everything, he told himself. Pain and pleasure. Better to burn up than to fade away.

An image came to him of the nervous system—no, his true love—standing by the bed, his head in flames. He suffered this image to remain, though a tiny sound broke from him; he heard it as if it were someone else's. Darling, his lover had signed, smiling, in so far as he could be said to smile. Oh, that was the killer, he didn't know he was burning. It was all one to him: flames, George's touch, a breath, laughter, death. What George felt about this: pity. Guilt. Also envy.

George passed among the nervous fibers in his birthday suit, going in deeper.

It could happen, thought George, he could rise again. A scattering of fibers that missed the hopper at harvest, a tidal wave of magnetized particles from the sun, a brief disturbance in the fields, and he could come again. Love's an accident waiting to happen.

The field began to hum.

# Shannon Holman
## HEAVEN

First we resumed our bodies. It was all there,
jarred and labeled—afterbirth, teeth (both sets),
nail clippings, effluvium, huge skeins of hair,
sloughed-off skin, and the cells
of every seven years, each set in its own jewel-case.

We coalesced, a documentary of leprosy run backwards.
It wasn't at all heavy, wearing our whole selves.
There we were, just as Paul promised: *impassible, bright, agile, subtle.*
We'd never looked so wonderful.

Next we rode bikes all around the great gates.
We sent up vast sprays of fall leaves, colors that, back in life,
we'd only seen in catalogs. We popped wheelies.
We had cards in our spokes—all royals,
famous historical figures, torch singers, ancestors,
whoever it was we wanted, pets included. Also trumpets
mounted on the handlebars, also tassels made of blond superstrings.

We were in a subjunctive mood. It lasted for years.

Then the gates swung open; we rode straight through
into the empty museum, wheels squeaking on the marble parquet,
into the Hall of VCRs, where history kicked its great legs
on a long row of flat-screen monitors. Then the diorama

explaining Human Suffering, then In My Image: A Portrait Gallery,
then the interactive map of the universe, drawn to scale.
At the end of the tour, a little placard asked us to kindly give Time back
along with our head-sets. We didn't mind. Everything was pluperfect.

In the fullness of time burst *Aloha!*

The big tent blazed and burned out, flamed and was doused.
He stood there in His striped coat, straight-back chair in His hand,
roaring, holding Himself back, padding, tawny, bare-back, remembering everything,
stumbling on the high-wire, swallowing fire, juggling knives, in knots,
He kept coming over and over out of that yellow VW.

# Henry Israeli
## FLAMINGOS

Flamingos fly southward, feathers pinkish-red
    as if they were tongues that could speak
with the dead. My father shuffles a deck
    of cards, cuts, then deals. The war rages on:
mud-soaked paramedics carrying the wounded
    on stretchers, scurrying through crossfire.
They leap up and become a flock of flamingos.
    My father touches my ear, calls me his little
*ptitchka*, his wounded wing. The cards smolder
    atop a mound of ashes; Nazis barking
orders on the manicured lawn wave
    blood-stained bayonets over the palms.
A flamingo, balanced on one leg, fills
    with red like a thermometer on the rise,
eyes expressionless, trained southward.
    Speak English, I say. Da? Da. I'm straining
to interpret his words, his peculiar gestures,
    when a hand-grenade lands on my lap.
I discretely place it on a bookshelf, pretend
    it never happened. I'm cracking open
a fresh deck, dealing the cards, poker-faced.
    The game is hearts. I can never win.

# Henry Israeli
## Newsreel

Still, sometimes, in carnage, a love
    savage and hemmed in the heartsleeve crops up:

two men, father and son, crawling across a field
of broken bones, knock foreheads, look up,
    wing-cocked gargoyles trapped in stone.

*You again?*

This happens more often than supposed.
At critical moments, one hardly notices the white sheet
    floating along the ceiling—

It's happened to us just now:
across the eternal landscape of language,
      missiles are flying. Take cover.

Her small grandson
sleeps curved against her, his face
pale as the moon, his breath fragrant
as night-blooming jasmine. With her hands,
she seeks to memorize his perfect body—
the feathery hair, boy-muscle of calf and bicep,
the track of his vertebrae—
so that years later she can summon up
every detail in her fingertips.

This started long ago,
this learning by heart the bodies of all the men
she slept beside. Not so much to recall
the particulars of them after their leaving,
but as a ritual in Braille, another way of knowing them
if ever they came back,
if ever she had to be sure of them in the dark.

# Christine Kuan

## COLLAGE POUR DADAMAX

*"das schlafzimmer des meisters es lohnt
sich darin eine nacht zu verbringen"*
—Max Ernst

what did you beget when you begot the autopilot
*sans le bourgeois*? little pumpkin fritter? little
robot? [the great orthochromatic wheel making
customized love] is an engine factory for hearts
to cut and cut or grate across the nubbly paper
like *frottage* from the fallen blood leaves gathered
on the woodgrain of [the horde]/ ominous antagonists.
plink plink [the fragrant forest] is a chest of torn wings
that fling over the border like two fingers of two legs.
when the arrow cracks [the robing of the bride] smells
complete like wet wax dripping sweet and peeling
for your *grattage* again raging hobby horse leaking
its own gouache. dada don't make mama with *decalcomania,*
pawn the refuse of misuse from [the bewildered planet]
for [one week of goodness]. oh still! stab her through
her foot with a dagger or look with your talon eyes at the
[two children threatened by the nightingale]. run
run Loplop for the two am i with elephant and a gent
en route to puberty dismembered and undressed/
[oedipus rex]!! thwarted disquiets and is raw and thaws
unschooled as you were probing, caving, swabbing
through the psycho *surréalisme* of the peg in the case.
tastes like a virgin spanking, an assortment of sweetbread
so ripe to be plucked like the [fruit of a long experience].

---

[1] *The master's bedroom it's worth spending a night there*. Collage (1919). Max Ernst.

# Susan Landers
## WHAT SHE GIVES HERSELF

She thinks about where to begin, beginnings being like that except once begun. To get out of this dark hall. A beginning is a frame of reference. To drink from a bottle. The head on her shoulders is a good one. She is seven and tired of being useful. To get out of this dark hall. She is two people. Today she isn't Ada. Today she isn't Mabel. When she is two people, she loses sight of her feet. To drink from a bottle. When the race is over, the exact shape doesn't matter. A horse is a horse. If Ada were inside, she'd knock on the door if there were a door between them. She is pleased to be in a conversation with Mabel. She signs the confession without leaving a mark. The words don't fit her. She thinks she could save the world a lot of trouble if she had more fits.

# Susan Landers

## Bomb Show

78

Femme fig.   Femme fish.   Fizz bomb
show femme.   Shrimp box. Fish for fish.
Femme for shrub film    fake bark feast
fib bosh.   Femme for shrink box.   (fair
shrew)    Bird for bird    Forge    fit
force. Shrug fate.   Femme botch fame
botch fib box    botch fire. Femme botch
fish box shrew.   (bad femme)    Shrew
shoot buff film    shoot fake farce. Box
shriek.   Shrew buck faith. Fetch shrewd
fame.   Fetch fate.   Shrew for fig bang
for bird bath    Shrew box fog    box fig.
Fish for fish.    Fish fair shrew for bad
fish    fair bird    for box box fetch fit.

Guess whose birthday it is
hint: his first name rhymes with felonious
and Keats wrote that
the imagination was his monastery
and he was its monk
I'll have that scotch straight, no chaser
and Joe will have his Pepsi with a twist
and Pepsi is the name of Emma McCagg's dog
where Joe and I are posing for a double portrait
this rainy afternoon of quietness
with Milt Jackson dead at 72
I may be too old to be a bohemian
but he was too young to die

# Timothy Liu
## UPDATE

Nor the closure that some wanted dressed in black.

Snack-pack pheno-barbital kicked-in by vodka shots.

As psychic hotline flacks beam down to Larry King.

Blood moon outside the holodeck Manson denied parole.

Millennial fever dissolving overheated cyber chat.

An enclave eucalyptus occasional coyote cries.

Permeating an immaculate house some stages of decay.

Or else loss of membership televisionary daze.

More credible than tabloid news recycled episodes.

A ghostly thermion whistling inside an inner ear.

Limbs as kitestick cruciform under purple shroud.

violations teething throaty laughs as juveniles take a blowtorch to that stray some sissies

hypnotized by a casual bulge reciting verses that Rumi wrote in praise of Shams buried

under mud that slid through windows nestled high on hills as footsteps of past masters fit

stifling masks onto pressed hams spied through shower glass in that parade of tongues

licking tender egos foisted onto thrones bejeweled with envy and regret where fat trolls

watch jocks peel off their shorts on that private beach fenced-in by porno stills unspooled

on the kitchen floor some hang-up calls the police can't trace as hurricanes come and go

# Timothy Liu
## PROTHALAMION

dawn's arrows poised for flight near banquet tables that run the entire length of heaven

while radio signals from alabama disrupt a late quartet haunted by squawks and jeers

that taunt us still all those frat boys wanting nothing but release their tattooed anchors

sinking beneath black light where disco reigns triumphant with death not far behind

our voices weak without the flesh without that white macaw and cockatoo chanting rote

affections asking us to pay attention where lights go down on love letters scrawled by

hand stacked shoulder-high to the wind as newlyweds now vanish behind a storm of rice

# Charlotte Mew

## FAME

Sometimes in the over-heated house, but not for long,
    Smirking and speaking rather loud,
    I see myself among the crowd,
Where no one fits the singer to his song,
Or sifts the unpainted from the painted faces
Of the people who are always on my stair;
They were not with me when I walked in heavenly places;
      But could I spare
In the blind Earth's great silences and spaces,
    The din, the scuffle, the long stare
    If I went back and it was not there?
Back to the old known things that are the new,
The folded glory of the gorse, the sweet-briar air,
To the larks that cannot praise us, knowing nothing of what we do
    And the divine, wise trees that do not care
Yet, to leave Fame, still with such eyes and that bright hair!
God! If I might! And before I go hence
      Take in her stead
      To our tossed bed,
One little dream, no matter how small, how wild.
Just now, I think I found it in a field, under a fence—
A frail, dead, new-born lamb, ghostly and pitiful and white,
      A blot upon the night,
      The moon's dropped child!

# Charlotte Mew
## THE TREES ARE DOWN

84

*—and he cried with a loud voice:*
*Hurt not the earth, neither the sea, nor the trees—*
                    (Revelation)


They are cutting down the great plane-trees at the end of the gardens.
For days there has been the grate of the saw, the swish of the branches as they fall,
The crash of trunks, the rustle of trodden leaves,
With the 'Whoops' and the 'Whoas,' the loud common talk, the loud
                              common laughs of the men, above it all.


I remember one evening of a long past Spring
Turning in at a gate, getting out of a cart, and finding a large dead rat
                              in the mud of the drive.
I remember thinking: alive or dead, a rat was a god-forsaken thing,
But at least, in May, that even a rat should be alive.

The week's work here is as good as done. There is just one bough
    On the roped bole, in the fine grey rain,
            Green and high
            And lonely against the sky.
                (Down now!—)
            And but for that,
            If an old dead rat

Did once, for a moment, unmake the Spring, I might never have

thought of him again.


It is not for a moment the Spring is unmade to-day;
These were great trees, it was in them from root to stem:
When the men with the 'Whoops' and the 'Whoas' have carted the

whole of the whispering loveliness away

Half the Spring, for me, will have gone with them.
It is going now, and my heart has been struck with the hearts of the planes;
Half my life it has beat with these, in the sun, in the rains,

In the March wind, the May breeze,
In the great gales that came over to them across the roofs from the great seas.

There was only a quiet rain when they were dying;
They must have heard the sparrows flying,
And the small creeping creatures in the earth where they were lying—

But I, all day, I heard an angel crying:

'Hurt not the trees.'

# Malena Mörling
## Wearing a Death

86

Not a dress, a death—
Not a coat, a coffin—
Not the sole of a shoe, a soul
that can't be glued to the underside of anything—

Wearing it the way you wear make-up
or a pair of eyeglasses—

Wearing it because you can't take it off
not even at night
to bathe
or sleep.

Tonight one half of the moon's face
    looks down
at us
    and our earthly secrets
that are invisible
      even in daylight—

Except in certain photographs
    where you might see something
commonplace
like laundry
flying high
over backyards in Queens or California
shirts hung in the sunlight with their sleeves down

or like plain water in a glass
      passing over the trembling lips
of a bedridden
    woman
    and swallowed in small gulps

    Or is it possible you'll glimpse in passing
a warm and loving exchange
    between two strangers
      reflected

for a single moment
in an ornate bureau mirror
traveling on a flatbed truck
        stopped at a red light here on 131st street—

I have never wanted to visit
                        outer space—

                        Though I have often thought
about how it never ends—

and how that is the reason a shoe is a secret

or a circus signboard is a secret
showing the four hooves of a horse
balancing on a painted red ball

or a leaf
or a hat
on the head
of a boy
or on the head of a woman riding the subway alone
                    into the evening
or for that matter the evening itself
as it gives way to night
and the night which is yet another secret
        as well as a garment
woven out of unnumbered fine black threads.

# Kathleen Ossip

## THE SIMP

FROM *24 Rants*

Cuando en el train, en el ghost train,
con los guns y los handbags, you drip
ice sweats. Cuando en la booth, you talk
long time. Some dumb hoodoo man dagnabbed
you for your sins! You ain't no psychic.
You ain't no shopper. Cuando en la
deli, you get a ham omelet.

# Kathleen Ossip

## THE ESSENTIALIST
FROM *24 Rants*

90

"This, this is what the dying are like!"
As I listened in the park I knew
there's nothing square about your sleek slide.
In the middle of the lake: "The soul
is violent. If it leaks at all,
it leaks in screams." Quel grand slam, quel null
set. It was to be a pleasure jaunt.

Tell her anything but be sure it's complementary.
Something like:
*We are separated siamese twins who have collected*
*the same morbid souvenirs. Ambidexterous*
*I write with your left hand.*

She will blush and your attention will be carried
up to her oval necklace. You will perceive
a sudden flaring up of love and then a sudden
dying down of it. The lover is apt to come across
a girl he thinks he loves who later turns out to be
only another person, her body once a temple
of calligraphy and giggling now a houseful of clocks
all set on different times with a sorrow in the middle
like a liquid center.

Listen to her hidden loudspeakers.
*All she wants to be is believed.*
Remember she is defenseless at breakfast,
always delicate and altered as if all night she's been
undergoing little surgeries.

Never go straight for her nipple.
Study instead her vaccination scar, circle it with
your finger, press it like an elevator button. As if

you were testing a cake for doneness, exert a gentle
pressure both culinary and religious. Her eyes
are little sliding glass doors and she fills you
with a colored helium and she fills your halls
with speechless people. Call her Katydid and Abode.
Turquoise patch on a bird's forehead.
Resurrection Plant.

You'll know you're doing it right if she says
*You make my heart soar like the cost of living*
if she tells you the species you freed near
her sternum is half fur-covered bird and half
feather-brained dog, swooping down to lick your face
her wing a clumsy paw, her clumsy paws the wings
she waits in for you to arrive—

And you won't question how the stem of one
flower can support a whole roof, you'll just pay
for your ticket and go on inside.

24TH AND 2ND AVE.

33RD AND 3RD AVE.

26TH AND 3RD AVE.

88TH AND WEST END AVE.

With all I've heard about A-bombs that'll destroy a city and H-bombs that'll destroy a state and chain reactions that'll destroy the world. . . you know I just don't have any incentive to buy a two pants suit.

RICHARD PRINCE
UNTITLED
ACRYLIC AND SILKSCREEN ON CANVAS
64⅝" x 48"

CROWD

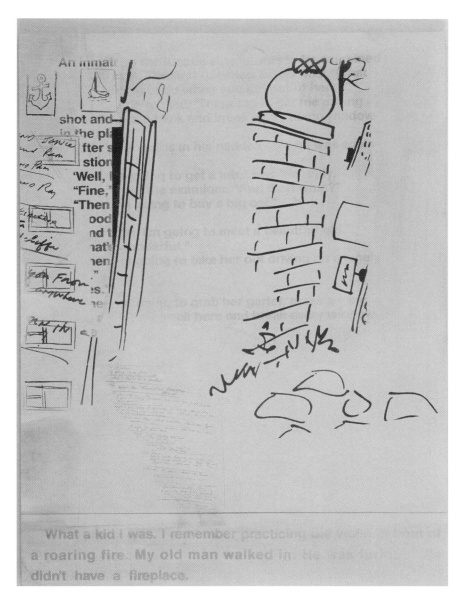

RICHARD PRINCE
TERRORIST OR FRIEND

ACRYLIC AND SILKSCREEN ON CANVAS
68" x 48"

RICHARD PRINCE
UNTITLED

ACRYLIC AND SILKSCREEN ON CANVAS
71" x 48"

CROWD

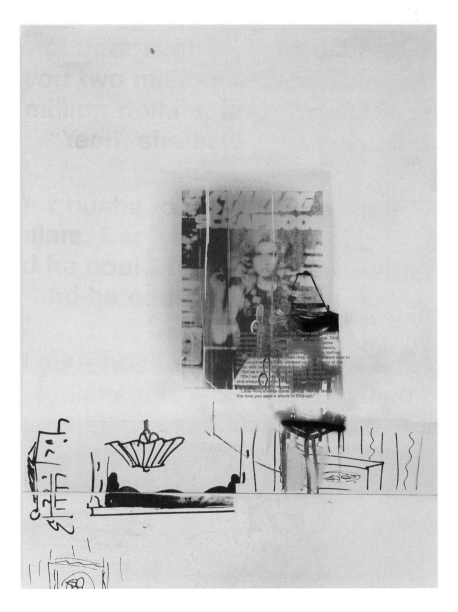

RICHARD PRINCE
TELL US ABOUT THE TIME YOU WERE A WHORE IN CHICAGO

ACRYLIC AND SILKSCREEN ON CANVAS
68" x 48"

Jay Gardner
Fall River, MA

Now move your broken sleep into the hallway and out the door,
down the path to the potato in the sand like an island.
To the edge of the ocean and its flotsam. This is where you always
come to thread your needles, wetting the ends of white silk
with saliva and shutting one eye.
In this secret sewing district it is always midwinter. Wind blows
through the window openings in your bones as if your skin
was a figment of your imagination.
Very often, if you count backwards from an arbitrary number
it will be exactly the same time when you return home
with dirty feet and a fish, but then you won't be able to remember
anything except the grunting sound it made when you took it
out of the water.

# Ravi Shankar

## BEFORE DREAMLAND BURNED DOWN IN CONEY ISLAND

Certainly it was splendid to see you again,
The trout on your pate was quite fetching,
And I did my best impression of fulfilling
Your dream of me: skittish, acerbic, sly.

The ditch I was pitched in proved to be a parlor,
The rattling prattle of folks for whom "callous"
Was an island in the Mediterranean.
I brought them drinks on a mirrored tray.

Along the heave of boardwalk, neon sliced
Evening into bite-size portions for squalid
Sailors and salacious pseudo-rodeo clowns.
An ebb of pleasure coterminous with despair.

And soon, as before, the wheel in the sky
Turned, my ear got caught on rope spoken
Through the barker's mouth while metal bottles
Toppled. Then you stole away the fish's eye.

# Hugh Steinberg
## GONE

Rise up in dreamyears, it's easy: the body shapes itself to the joy it needs. Rise up in sparks, I'll get the sparks straight and drive an Impala! To Reno! Nevada! I'll grow my hair as long as Rene DesCartes! I'll get a Chevy and forget about lingering, I'll be heartless gone, fall asleep kind of gone! So I took my legs and used up my life, I'll buy another one! I'll buy it at Sears! I'll wear the clothes of mechanical engineers! I'll leave my heart in its sockets, I'll zip condoms into each of my pockets, I'll give my mother up to the police! Nothing will bring me back! I'll teach my own heart how to contract! I'll make twenty bucks an hour just to hear you confess! So what if your hand undoes each knot, if it smokes laughter, if it stays bought? Oh how you tipped me! I could never get up! I had to get rid of my body I just ditched it! The things you throw down you lie down upon or you sleep standing up and without me! So look, under these grids of stone, the countlight, the headlight, the light which carries, millionvoiced and arguing, I got so continual in your consequences, I had to go! There were wasps above us, a crown of wings endlessly beating! They said heartsound gone, they said all kinds of gone! The shattered world, the shadowed world, overlapping your world, it ain't my world! I was never sad! I was never sad!

# Virgil Suárez
## El Arabe

Or *El Musúlman*, as everyone in our neighborhood called him.
Nobody really knew where he was from, though some said
Lebanon, or Syria, but his skin was dark and his eyes glowed

whenever he walked down our street at night. He smoked
pungent cigars, *maduros*, and the smell lingered behind him
long after he'd disappeared. Some nights you could hear him

chanting a song in Arabic. Mournful and devastating. Some
say he lost his wife and family back home, or on the trip
out here to Cuba. My grandmother spoke to him once.

He held her hands and looked into her eyes, smiled, winked
then he bowed to kiss her palms. Nobody but me saw them.
He predicted many things, having chosen to stay in Havana

even after the revolution. Some say he knew things never
would be the same with the country, with its people. Yet
everyday he walked by, once in the afternoon, once past dusk.

Nobody knew where he went to or where he came from.
Whenever he walked down our street, we shouted out to him:
*Arabe! Arabe! Arabe!* He walked on with the elegance of days

gone by, Casablanca days. Some say *El Arabe* is still there,
in Havana, going by twice. His eyes two firefly flashes,
in his hands the burning cigar, him singing mournful songs.

# Matthew Thorburn

## Two Lives

*–for Hilda LaMoreaux (1974-1999)*

I ducked out of *Three Sisters* at intermission, feeling too
conspicuous, too out of place there alone,
so up and out
                        and walked down Whitehall Street, thinking of you,
and wandered round Trafalgar Square—alone.

I wanted to walk back all the way to Wood Green, where
you used to live
                        with Rosie, your Italian flat-mate, under low
ceilings, bare bulbs, the water too cold for washing hair—

to say (too late), Forgive my reticence, my infrequent calls, how
it seemed sometimes I lived
                                two lives, pushing on in one,
one circling back to re-imagine and rearrange

what happened and what might have—
                                        details one
by one assembled into another life that's good (for poetry),
                                                    but strange
and not quite mine.
                        So this play stays, like so much else, half-finished,
the mystery—you'd say *wonder*—
                                of what comes next undiminished.

The man sat with a pint of bitter on the patio of McGuirk's, looking out on the thumbprint of the shore. The sand reflected so brightly that it hurt to look at it. He was nearly blind in this light. When I finish, he decided, I will walk out to the afternoon tide to check the feeling in my legs. He did not mind watching the young girls walk past in bathing-suit tops, the half moon of their breasts showing. He was not an old man, only in his late twenties, only the age of some of the women that strolled the boardwalk still looking fit. But his body had aged on him.

He had grown up in a beach town in Virginia, had spent his childhood summers on the boardwalk and in the waves. He remembered the feeling of the warm tidal pool. The water was calm, tepid, and there was a piece of driftwood that floated about. His mother worried over him playing in the standing water. She coaxed him away, out to the breaking surf. The sand rushed from beneath his feet and the water treaded back. The feeling of the sand going made him dizzy, and he could not look down.

"The water is fine," his mother said. "You'll get used to it once you're in."

He worried about what he couldn't see beneath the surface. His mother held his hand. They walked out until the water was at his waist and he saw that the waves swelled, rose up higher than his head.

"Jump!" his mother called. And they both jumped, and the water carried them up high and washed them in closer to the beach. The boy laughed. "Wasn't that fun!" she said. He nodded.

The boy's fear slowly immersed itself with each passing wave. The cold water felt good on his face, the swells pushing him about nicely. His mother let go of his hand, and they both jumped together into each wave. Far off, in the distance, he thought he could see an island. He wondered how difficult it would be to swim there. Maybe Olympic swimmers could swim there, he thought. I bet Mark Spitz could swim there. He saw a big wave moving toward them.

"Here comes a big one," his mother called. "Hold my hand." But she was too far away and the current was too much. "Jump!" she finally called.

The wave carried him for a while and left him on his feet. It was the most pleasant thing. It was like walking on the moon, he thought, the wave taking you gently over the ground. His mother was still out in the water, where they both had been standing together. The boy stood laughing.

"Go in!" the mother yelled. "Go in!"

It wasn't clear to the boy what she meant. She seemed upset, but why? The water was barely above his knees. He smiled. "What's wrong?" he called back.

"Go farther in!" she cried.

The boy waded toward her, looking out at the rising surf. This one will take me even farther, he thought. He pushed hard, wanting to make it into the surge.

"The other way!" his mother cried.

He looked up. He would not make the wave, but rather the break. He turned away, tried to high step. The breaker caught him, threw him face first. His head hit the bottom, hard. He went black for a moment, then felt his body tumble, scrape across the ocean floor. It was as though someone had taken sandpaper to his arms and legs and forehead. He sucked in water, began to choke. The water rolled him for what seemed a long time. Then he was left terrified, thirty yards down the beach. A lifeguard reached him first. His mother was crying. He had lain around the house for days, his mother putting medicine on his scrapes. She worried about infection. He was diabetic. His head ached, his injuries burned. He had gotten a slight concussion and one of the abrasions would scar. It was still visible on his shoulder.

Clouds rose high up in the distance. It will rain later, he thought as he finished his beer. He left five dollar coins on the table, descended the steps to the street. Down the avenue there were noisy arcades, young boys and girls beginning their lifelong affair with gambling. There were tacky clothing shops and a strip casino where old men went in their guayaberas and baggy shorts. Straw Panamas, scrunched down, blocked the sun. The man did not like the bustle, so he crossed the street so that he could walk along the beach. The sand would work his muscles.

My right leg needs work, he thought. I should have gone for therapy after the injury. He had been building bookshelves. He had stained the white pine planks. There were so few tools in the house. This building notion was new. But he'd read about building shelves and was enticed by the photographs. Most of his books had been in storage for a few years. He'd finished his schooling—his doctorate from M.I.T.—not more than a few years before. But when he was done there were no jobs for him at the universities. He took a job as a night assistant on an eighty-seven-inch telescope out west. He loved the cool, breezy, nighttime work. But in the day he was free and secluded. The next town was an hour and half away. So he decided on a handyman pastime. He thought, I'll take out my books, maybe begin my own research on UV-Ceti stars. There is plenty of free time on the small telescopes. I could do the work during full moon. So he bought lumber. He wanted to countersink the screws. His drill was cheap, with only one bit, so he used screws to make the holes. He didn't have a bench and he drilled through, easily, into his foot. At first he did not know. He bore the second hole and then noticed blood on the floor. He went to lift the plank, but couldn't. It was screwed into his foot. His drill didn't have reverse, so he had to sidestep to his toolbox, where he used a screwdriver. It wasn't until then that he took account of how much feeling he had lost.

He had been diabetic his entire life. They called this lack of feeling neuropathy. But it wasn't just numbness. It was both numbness and it was shooting pain. The arching pain came at night—rhythmic, sharp pulses that worked like torture. It was pain that could keep him from sleeping for days at a time. His not sleeping was the added factor in the mistake, in his drilling a hole in his own foot. The only thing that kept him sane was his night work on the telescope. It kept him from thinking about his illness, about the fact that slowly he was losing contact with the world.

His deck shoes were full of sand, he was sure, but he could not feel it. Far out on the horizon a sailboat tossed in the waves. The lifeguards had gone home, their towers having been dragged across the sand and stored near the boardwalk. He followed their tracks in the sand. He pushed hard, working his leg. For two years he had been on crutches. Several doctors had wanted to amputate, but finally he found one in Boston who could help. The doctor had saved his leg. Gulls hovered, dipped. Some pecked at the surf's edge, their black-tipped beaks coming up with food. The beach was changing hands. Mostly, the fat, old, afternoon crowd had replaced the young tan bodies. A few muscled, T-shirted boys tossed a frisbee. Really, the young crowd had gone home to shower and dress for the seaside bars. The man knew he could find people his own age at the Sea Breeze. But he did not feel his own age. He thought of the crowd at the casino.

The man pushed on through the sand for a quarter mile. He felt the muscles in his legs tighten. I have to be careful not to push too hard, he thought. I'll walk down close to the water. So he did. The water rolled up onto the beach, smoothing the sand out like wet cement. Overhead a plane bannered across the sky, "The Sea Wok, Best Chinese in Town." Who comes to the beach for Chinese, he thought. He even laughed out loud at this. Far out on the peninsula he could see where the cheap motels gave way to condos, then to large, rich houses. At the point was a lighthouse. Its beacon was already clearly visible in the afternoon light. The man thought of how he couldn't make enough money.

The universities didn't want a sick man, a man with a disability. They asked questions and then told him they were sorry but he did not meet their needs. A night assistant makes nothing, he thought. It's only enough to live on and occasionally take a vacation such as this. There are no towns, no places to spend money near the observatory. But there are professors living in the rich houses on the peninsula, he thought. He thought of the observatory, the white domes. He had spent the better part of his life looking at the smallest patch of sky, only what could be seen through the shuttered opening of the dome. He had all but forgotten the constellations. I have all but forgotten what it is like to live in the world, he thought. Ahead of him, he could see a sizable group of young people, huddled. He walked to them and stopped. They were laughing, shoveling sand.

"Did you bury him standing up?" the man asked. The boy was maybe eight, perhaps short for his age.

"Yeah," one of the girls answered, the straps of her swimsuit down, off her shoulders.

"Do you think that's a good idea?" he asked.

"Why not?" the girl said.

"The tide."

"What about it?"

"It's coming in," he said. He pointed out to the waves. They were coming in hard on the sand.

"Mind your own business, mister," the buried boy said.

The man looked at the boy. "Suit yourself," he said. He walked down the beach a little way and then decided to wade out into the surf. It was late summer and the water should have been cold. The water streamed over his feet and he felt nothing. He waded out a little farther, until the water broke at his knees. He only felt the push of the surf. The boys and girls of the group were laughing. He turned to watch.

They took photographs of the buried boy, only his head showing. They had packed the sand around him so that not even his neck showed. The man noticed that some of the boys had T-shirts on with the letters "W.W.J.D.?" They are a church group, the man thought. He knew the Letters. He'd heard about it on the radio. "What Would Jesus Do?" The girls were modest, towels wrapped at their waists. A girl dropped her towel, kneeled, and kissed the boy for a photograph. The boy howled.

The man waded farther out, until the water was at his stomach, and only then did he feel the slightest tingle of the cold water. Is the feeling real, he thought, or am I just imagining? He dipped his hands in and felt nothing with them. The man could not hear the church group any longer, just the ocean and the sound of a Hood blimp that drifted overhead. The white-and-red balloon glided effortlessly, only a hundred feet overhead. What a wonderful feeling, the man thought. I would like to see the beach from there. It must look like a cuticle. It must be like the smallest sliver of the moon, but with people gathered at the cusp. It made him remember an Italo Calvino story, where people would row a cork boat into the sea, lean a ladder up, and climb onto the moon. The blimp hovered for a few minutes and then headed out over the water, toward the rich houses that stood solemn and white.

The man waded farther out, to his chest. The rising current still scared him. With each wave that came, he jumped and was carried. Really only his face felt the cold water. The glare of the afternoon still left him almost blind. He looked upward at the blue sky and could see the scars left by hemorrhages. He had lost a great deal of sight. But he still had his sense of smell, and he loved the salt and the freshness of each wave. He tried to feel everything he could. He tried to body surf each wave, but it only made him unhappy. He wished to be a child again, to feel the pain of the breaking waves. After a while he made his way back to the shore. He lay on the sand, just out of reach of the water.

He heard a boy scream. Down the beach he could see that a wave had made it up to where the boy was buried. The sand had gone smooth and dark. Several of the older boys were working frantically with the shovel, taking turns.

"Hurry up!" he yelled. "Goddamn it, hurry up!" He was crying.

Each wave that came in carried more sediment. The water turned the sand to wet cement and the boys were working against time. The man thought about running for help. He thought, I should go for help. But then he didn't. He thought of the boys with the letters on their T-shirts. "Mind your own business," the buried boy had said.

"God, please help me!" the boy screamed. A wave rushed in and over his head. By now all of the group were working with their hands and feet. One older man was pulling on the boy's arms. The boy screamed with pain. Another wave rushed over him. He coughed and sputtered. "Help me, somebody!" he screamed. "Get me out of here."

The man did not look. He stared out at the ocean. He thought he could see an island far off on the horizon. A sailboat tipped by and he was certain there was an island. By now all of the members of the church group were yelling, working frantically. The tide was rising quickly. The boy's screams had gone wordless. They were just random noises, like the gulls squawking out over a fish kill. The man looked and could see a wake in the sand, where the water rushed back. It was like the trace a motorboat made far out in the ocean. Soon it would be gone. The tide broke heavily on the beach, the waves rushing up and over the man's legs and lap. He thought of the girl kissing the boy and the photograph. He thought of his mother holding his hand, of the scar on his shoulder. Soon the boy's yelling would cease. The tide rushed over his body, up to his chest. Still, I cannot feel the water, he thought. The tide rushed over him and he had almost no feeling.

# Marina Wilson
## GROWING UP WITH MILK: AN APOLOGY

112

Growing up with you
was never easy, Milk.
When I reached for your hand,
your fingers slipped through mine.
I was always asking, why so blue, Milk?
Milk, you couldn't climb fences and didn't like to get your feet dirty.
I wanted you to be wild, Milk. You became my primary obsession.
The snow was you, Milk, in fragments that melted against my skin.
The curve of the moon was you, Milk, turning your back on me—Milk,
everything was you. The ticking of the clock
was you too.

The refrigerator hummed through the night.
The salt in its shaker waited neatly on the table.
The water went on running in circles.

I wanted you wild, Milk.

Instead, you fed me static.
You stuffed cotton down my throat.
It's all in the thickness, you said.

But you said so many things, Milk.

"...un quartier urbain n 'est pas déterminé par les facteurs géographiques et économiques mais par la représentation que ses habitants et ceux des autres quartiers en ont..."
Chombart de Lauwe,as quoted in
*Théorie de la Dérive* ,by G.Debord.(1956)

A monument is meant to serve a community of people, working as a physical reminder of the myths and stories that construct a collective identity. Traditionally neo-classical in style, they tend to take the form of stone, columnar giants and are highlighted with expensive lighting. Natural monuments however, have an innate story or presence that pre-dates their designation as a monument. An example of this might be the internally monumental Muir Woods, north of San Francisco.

I live in Berlin. The city itself is a kind of a human-made, "natural" monument. So many defining events of the last century occurred here that even Daniel Liebeskind, the architect of Berlin's new Jewish Museum, couldn't draw enough axes to connect them all. The residue of three major wars—two hot and one cold—as well as the confrontation of radically differing ideologies over a long span of time has left a city full of hundreds of reminders of its past. If you look at the texture of the city today, you will notice that things here are either new and shiny, or extremely old. Not old like Egypt or Mazatlán but rather a "contemporary" old, an old which feels like it's at the far edge of how long you can hold your breath. The old things that happened here are still relevant today, while the new is so new, sometimes I'm wary of walking on the sidewalk, or running my hand down the railing of the subway stairs, because the guy working there just finished packing up his tools and is walking away to smoke a cigarette and drink a hefeweissen.

Proposing that Berlin is this type of living "natural" monument, leads me to wonder how the daily movements and experiences of an individual's life in the city define and redefine personal monuments for a single person. Most personal

114

monuments have nothing to do with history at all, but are composed of a series of urban fragments synergized from a particular individual's experiences. For me, Berlin is both city and living icon. Here I thought I would share the kinds of monuments which "scale" Berlin to the personal level, making it possible to grasp the presence of the city's history, its identity, and mine within it.

HOW TO USE THIS PROJECT:

The following personal monuments were visited during a single day, the 20th of April 2001. Attached to each image you will find the following information:
1.   TIME-INDEX CODE (exact time I visited)
2.   ADDRESS/SHORT DESCRIPTION
3.   TRAPDOOR (how to contact my monument)
4.   DETAILS about the monument

8.10

ackerstraße 169 **my bedroom**

www.thinkbuild.com

My bedroom, roughly 5m x 7m, is my base. I spent just about all of my free time during the month of March working on the place, ripping and pulling, tearing, and painting, and now, it is a landmark, well on its way to becoming a (personal) monument.

9.10

ackerstraße 169 **my bicycle**

+1 413/585.8833

A mobile monument, my bike serves as much more than just my transport; it is my medium to understand the city. It has served this purpose for me in three major cities: Boston, NYC, and now, Berlin. The contact number is for the shop I bought it in, *Competitive Edge*, in Hadley, Massachusetts.

9.27

schönhauser 23-25 **the jewish cemetary**

+49 30/9.25.33.30

Built in 1827 by Berlin's flourishing Jewish community and destroyed by the Nazis before WWII, the cemetary sits as a melencholy witness to Berlin's loss. It contains hundreds of overturned gravestones, vandalized some 60-odd years ago, during the Battle of Berlin.

10.12

alexanderplatz **the wurst-o-nauts**

+49 30/427.7161

Every city has its urban cyborgs—Paris with its *caveliers de la merde*, (guys in green leather on vacuum-equipped motorcycles collecting dog shit), NYC with its roasted nut-men, and Berlin with its *Grillwalkers*. These jet-pack-powered, sausage-frying salesmen's natural habitat is in the most unnatural environment possible: Alexanderplatz.

11.15

museumsinsel **the gate of ishtar**

+49 30/20.90.55.77

Constructed between 604 and 562BC, the Gate of Ishtar has got to be the oldest of Berlin's monuments, albiet a borrowed one. A piece of a monument rebuilt in a monumental museum which collects monuments, the gate with its huge and gorgeous "Mushhushshus" (dragons), was discovered, uncovered, and shipped to Berlin's Pergamon Museum between 1899 and 1917.

11.36

niederkirchner straße **the wall**

+49 30/254.5090

Sitting on the boundary of the *Topographie des Terrors*, this half-eaten piece of the wall is one of the last remaining in the city. I remember this place clearly from my first visit to Berlin, when I visited the exhibit there about the former SS-torture chambers which were right under the foundations of the wall.

12.32
kastinienallee 89 **kamun falafel shop**

One night this winter I went to Kamun at about 2AM on a very cold Tuesday. The man behind the counter looked at me and asked if I wanted a lentil soup. "Yes, that's exactly right," and then we were quiet... I eating, he cleaning. His girlfriend came in and he broke into a 5km smile and the two disappeared in the back, leaving me alone with the slowly rotating doner and my soup.

13.14
kastinienallee 17 **vokuhila**
+49 30/44.34.25.13

"*Vorner kurz, Hinten lang*"—"short in the front, long in the back," *Vokuhila* offers the classic mullet, free of charge to those who dare. This is one of those funky regular businesses in Prenzlauerberg, which according to the story used to be a chop-shop in the DDR and became re-appropriated post-wall by local hipsters.

13.47
fehrbellerstrasse 25 **eisen-werner**
+49 30/449.0070

Since 1919, the Werner family has offered some of the best screws in Berlin. It's rare to find a shop where the guy behind the counter will take half an hour to discuss with you the installation details of the lock he is selling you, count all 46 of the 15mm bolts you need and then ask if you need another filter for the dust mask you bought two months ago.

14.21
veteranenstraße 25 **bergstüb'l bar**
+49 173/870.7128

Bergstüb'l is the most archetypical bar of all Berlin Bars: the bar that opened just last week. Going out in Berlin you develop patterns, becoming a regular in certain places. Simulateously, there is a pull to go to the new place, which is of course always just around the corner from the old one, not really better or cleaner but just slightly newer in that old Berlin way.

14.54
invalidienstraße 3 **elisabethkirche**
+49 30/308.7920

Built by Karl Friedrich Schinkel in 1835, this little gem of a church was bombed during WWII. It then sat, overgrown and romantic, exemplifying that most elegant of urban ruins: the church with no roof. Over the years I climbed the fence more then a few times, and always had fantasies about this wonderous and forgotten space in the middle of Berlin. It is under partial renovation at the moment and I fear for its romatic remains.

15.10
rhienhardstrasse 3 **bunker**

I took a photo of this bunker during the summer of 1997, in preparation for my Master's Thesis. It was a detail shot—of a bullet hole in the façade—and I am pretty sure it was then that I understood how the whole of Berlin is a monument. This building, like many other bunkers throughout Germany, is so solid (bomb-proof in fact), that there is nothing they can do about it: it's too solid (concrete) to remove it, change it, or renovate it: it's an accidentally permanent monument, natural, if you will.

15.15
betrtolt brecht platz 1
**berliner ensemble**
+49 30/284.080

The Berliner Ensemble was Bertolt Brecht's theater. Here is where *The Threepenny Opera* was first preformed and it was the original political cabaret of Kurt Weill.

16.10
freidrichstrasse
**hilmar schmundt & desk**
www.spiegel.de

Sometimes I feel like Berlin chose me more than that I chose Berlin. Cities sometimes have that effect but often you can trace the cause to a cites' human agent; in this case, geographer/journalist Hilmar Schmundt. Seated in his office at *Der Spiegel*, (The Mirror), Hilmar Schmundt smiles out at me and the world.

17.15
potsdamer str. 50 **neue nationalgalerie**
+49 30/20.90.55.55

Built by Mies van der Rohe in 1963, the Neue Nationalgalerie is a monument to the right angle as well as to art. A major component of the Kulturforum, the famously recognized floating roof actually contains only half of the total exhibition space.

17.26
potsdammer str. 33-37 **the staatsbib-liotek**
+49 30/26.60

You will see this room in Wim Wender's *Wings of Desire*. It's the room where the Angels walk around, listening to peoples' internal thoughts. Perhaps the greatest standing masterwork of Berlin architecture, Hans Scharoun built a temple to the mind, a library of culture for a city recovering from war.

17.43
savigny platz 11 **schutick**
www.schutick.de

Known for expensive but badly designed shoes, I clearly remember buying a pair of shoes here in 1992. At the time, there were no chichi shops in East Berlin where I was living; as such, I viewed Savignyplatz and in particular Shutick as a kind of Berlin outpost of chichiness. Shutick hasn't changed much, but Berlin has.

19.50
strausburger platz 12 **liza's kitchen**

Invited for dinner, Liza forcefully reminds me that her kitchen would be a monument in *any* city. Liza, who is both an American (from Arkansas), and an architect, has made a space which for me, is a kind of safe-spot, offering during every visit not only delicious culinary delights but also strange Turkish music and delectable conversation.

ANDY RYAN
UNTITLED

$3\frac{3}{5}$" x $5\frac{1}{2}$"

ANDY RYAN
UNTITLED

4" x 4⅝"

STEVEN A. HELLER
49TH FLOOR

# Contributor's Notes

**Robert Archambeau**'s books include *Word Play Place* (Swallow) and *Citation Suite* (Wild Honey). He is the editor of the international poetry review *Samizdat*, and teaches at Lake Forest College. He recently edited *Vectors: New Poetics*, which will be published by Samizdat Editions this fall.

**John Beer** lives in Chicago and teaches at Robert Morris College.

**Debbie Benson** is from North Canton, Ohio and is a graduate poetry student in New York City.

**Laure-Anne Bosselaar** is the author of *The Hour Between Dog and Wolf*. Her second poetry collection, *Small Gods of Grief*, won the Isabella Gardner Prize for Poetry for 2001. She is the editor of *Outsiders: Poems about Rebels, Exiles and Renegades* and *Urban Nature: Poems about Wildlife in the City*.

**Joe Brainard & Ron Padgett**: In the fall of 1963, artist Joe Brainard and poet Ron Padgett, both 21 years old, did a series of small collaborative works on card stock, typing paper, and tracing paper: drawings, words, and collaged material, much of it rather cryptic and hysterical, some of it erotic, some of it appropriating images from comic strips. Their working method was highly collaborative; that is, Brainard added some words and Padgett added some images. Using the limited media and materials at hand, the two worked spontaneously at a kitchen table in Padgett's living room, passing the pieces back and forth, drinking coffee, chuckling, and smoking. Over four or five such sessions, they ended up with around sixty pieces, four of which are included in this issue. Joe Brainard's work is the subject of a major traveling retrospective (at PS 1 September 30-December 30, 2001). Ron Padgett's most recent collection is *Poems I Guess I Wrote* (Cuz Editions).

**Rafael Campo** teaches and practices general internal medicine at Harvard Medical School and Beth Israel Deaconess Medical Center in Boston. His newest book, *Diva* (Duke University Press, 1999), written with the support of a Guggenheim fellowship, was a finalist for the National Book Critics Circle Award, the Paterson Poetry Prize, and a Lambda Literary Award. Other poems from his next collection have appeared recently or are forthcoming in *Black Book*, *Callaloo*, *The New England Review*, *The New Republic*, *Slate*, *TriQuarterly*, *The Western Humanities Review*, and elsewhere.

**Shanna Compton**'s poetry has appeared in *Borderlands*, *elimae*, *Santa Barbara Review*, and elsewhere. She lives in Brooklyn.

**Kevin Cooley** is a graduate of the School of Visual Arts MFA program in Photography and Related Media. His work explores the world of the 'semi-private'. The photos featured here highlight boundaries between the public streets and the private interiors of parked cars. Kevin received the David Ruttenberg Purchase Award, the Paula Rhodes Memorial Award, and the Aaron Siskind Memorial Scholarship. His work has been displayed as a part of the MFA Photography Thesis Exhibition at Anthology Film Archives, at the Visual Arts Gallery, the Angel Orensanz Foundation, the Helmsley Spear Galleries and the Elaine Benson Gallery.

**Michael Costello** is from upstate New York.

**Lynn Crosbie** is a Toronto writer. Her last book is *Queen Rat: New and Selected Poems*. "Roach French Fries" previously appeared in *The IV Lounge Reader*.

**Jason Danziger** is an architect currently teaching design in urban contexts at the Technisches Universitaet in Berlin, Germany. He has studied, among other things, cooking (and eating), languages, sculpture and photography. He received his M. Arch. from the Massachusetts Institute of Technology in February 1998.

**Connie Deanovich** is the author of *Zombie Jet* (Zoland Books) and *Watusi Titanic* (Timken). A Whiting Writer's Award recipient, she lives in Madison Wisconsin.

**Geoffrey DeTrani** is an artist and writer living in New York. His poetry and prose has appeared in several publications including *Crossconnect* and *NY Arts Magazine*. His artwork is in the collections of the Museum of Modern Art and the Brooklyn Museum of Art.

Trane Devore is from Rescue, California, graduated from Sonoma, and is currently working on a doctorate in English at the University of California, Berkeley. His work has appeared in *Tight*, *Prosodia*, *Mirage*, and the late *Exquisite Corpse*, among others, and is the author of a book, *series/mnemonic* (Avec Books, 1999). He has work forthcoming in *First Intensity* and *Chain*. In his spare time Trane draws comics, takes photographs, and plays the clarinet.

Ray DiPalma's books include *Letters* (Littoral Books), *Provocations* (Potes & Poets Press), and *Motion of the Cypher* (Roof Books). New poems have been published in issues of *Cross-Cultural Poetics*, *Parataxis*, *First Intensity*, *Verse*, *Chicago Review*, and *APR*. He lives in New York City and teaches at the School of Visual Arts.

Denise Duhamel's most recent poetry collection is *Queen for a Day: Selected and New Poems* (University of Pittsburgh Press, 2001). An assistant professor at Florida International University in Miami, she is the recipient of a 2001 National Endowment for the Arts Fellowship in Poetry.

Mary Donnelly is a Brooklyn-based poet, screenwriter and video producer. Her poetry has appeared in *Open City*, *Nerve*, and *Bleach*. She is Co-Director of the "Reading Between A&B" poetry series in New York City and is currently in the MFA Writing Seminars program at Bennington College.

MK Francisco lives in Seattle where she edits *Scout Magazine* and attends the University of Washington. Her recent work appears or is forthcoming in *Outlet*, *580 Split*, *Fence* and *Quarterly West*.

Jay Gardner invented the ink-transfer process while a student in New York in the mid-1990's. His current work focuses on the interpretation through historical memory of both urban and rural subjects and can be seen at *www.jaygardner.com*. He lives in New York and Massachusetts.

Jane Hammond was educated at Mt. Holyoke College and the University of Wisconsin at Madison. She moved to New York City in 1980. In 1989 the first solo show of her paintings was mounted at Exit Art in New York. Since then she has had seven solo exhibitions in New York and other solo exhibitions in Stockholm, Amsterdam, Barcelona, Milan, Detroit, Chicago, Seattle and Kansas City. Solo museum exhibitions have been organized at the Honolulu Academy of Art, at the Cincinnati Museum of Art, and at the Orlando Museum of Art. Her paintings have been written about in the *New York Times,* the *Los Angeles Times*, *Art in America*, *The New Yorker*, *Artforum*, *Modern Painters*, *Art News*, *Art & Antiques*, *The Village Voice*, *FlashArt*, *Arts Magazine* and many other publications. She is the recipient of the Louis Comfort Tiffany Foundation Grant, the Ludwig Vogelstein Foundation Grant in Painting, two New York State Council on the Arts Grants, the National Endowment for the Arts Fellowship and the Joan Mitchell Foundation Grant Award. Galerie Lelong represents Ms. Hammond.

**124**

**Kristen Hanlon**'s poems have recently appeared in *Colorado Review*, *Fourteen Hills*, and *VOLT*. Last year she received the James D. Phelan Award from the San Francisco Foundation for her manuscript-in-progress, currently titled *Near Life Experience*. She lives in Oakland, California.

**Harrrison Haynes** was born in North Carolina. He received a BFA in Painting from the Rhode Island School of Design and currently lives in Brooklyn. His recent watercolors can be seen at Bellwether Gallery in Williamsburg, Brooklyn.

**Steven A. Heller**'s photographs have appeared in *Blind Spot*, *Graphis*, *Time*, *The Los Angeles Times Magazine*, *Metropolis*, *Details*, *Blur*, *I.D.*, and *Business Week* among other publications. He has won awards from the Type Directors Club, *Communication Arts*, *Print*, The 100 Show, American Institute of Graphic Artists (AIGA), and the American Federation for the Arts. He has worked as photographer for the College at Art Center College of Design in Pasadena since 1986, and in 1991 was named Photographer of the Year by The Council for the Advancement and Support of Education (CASE). Heller's fine art photography has been exhibited at the Gallery for Contemporary Photography in Santa Monica, the Center for Exploratory and Perceptual Art in Buffalo, New York, Soho Triad Fine Art Gallery in New York, and both the Mendenhall Gallery and Art Center College of Design in Pasadena.

**Shannon Holman** accepts the fluster in Brooklyn.

**Henry Israeli**'s collection, *New Messiahs*, will be published by Four Way Books in 2002. *Fresco: Selected Poetry of Luljeta Lleshanaku*—which he edited and co-translated—will be realeased by New Directions in the spring of 2002. A playwright as well, Henry Israeli lives in New York with his wife and daughter.

**Shelley Jackson** <*ineradicablestain.com*> is the author of the hypertext novel *Patchwork Girl*. Her fiction has appeared in numerous print and electronic journals, including *Grand Street*, *Fence* and *Conjunctions*. She has also written and illustrated several books for children. Her story collection, *The Melancholy Of Anatomy*, will be published by Anchor in Spring 2002.

**Lois Klein** has been writing and teaching poetry in the California Poets in the Schools project in Santa Barbara for the last decade. She received an Excellence in Writing Award from the Santa Barbara Writers Conference in 1997 and has been published in *The Lucid Stone*, *After Hours*, and the *Santa Barbara Independent*. Her chapbook, *Naming Water*, was published in 1998.

**Kuling** was born and raised in New York City where she lives, working as a photographer and cinematographer.

**Christine Kuan** recently moved from Iowa back to New York City and works at The Metropolitan Museum of Art.

**Susan Landers** lives in Brooklyn where she edits the journal *Pom²*.

**David Lehman** teaches in the core faculty of the graduate writing programs at the New School in New York and at Bennington College in Vermont. His most recent book of poems is *The Daily Mirror* (Scribner, 2000). He is the series editor of *The Best American Poetry* anthology and is co-director of the Monday night poetry reading series at the KGB Bar in New York City.

**Timothy Liu**'s latest book of poems is *Hard Evidence* (Talisman House, 2001). New work is forthcoming in *Ploughshares*, *TriQuarterly* and *The Yale Review*.

**Charlotte Mew** (1869-1928) was called "the greatest living poetess" by Virginia Woolf, and Thomas Hardy praised her as "far and away the best living woman poet—who will be read when others are forgotten." Though Mew, who committed suicide in 1928, is no household name, her work is experiencing a revival in England, and by reprinting two of her poems here, we hope to revive her poetry on this side of the Atlantic as well.

**Matthew Monteith** lives and works in New York City. He studied at the International Center of Photography and will be working on a Fulbright fellowship in the Czech Republic this fall. The images here are from two artist's books, *Glimpse* (from a voyage through Japan) and *Disquiet* (an examination of public spaces in New York). He is an annual participant in La Saison Photographique in Cherbourg, France. His work has been published in *Fortune*, *Details*, *US* and *The New York Times Sunday Magazine*.

**Malena Mörling**'s book of poems *Ocean Avenue* received The New Issues Press Poetry Prize in 1999. She is currently teaching in the MFA Writing Program at Syracuse University.

**Kathleen Ossip**'s poetry has been published or is forthcoming in *The Paris Review*, *The Antioch Review*, *Fence*, *Barrow Street*, *Slope.org*, and other journals. One of her poems appears in *The Best American Poetry 2001*, and she teaches a poetry workshop at The New School.

**Christa Parravani** is a second year MFA student in Photography at Columbia University and lives in Manhattan. She has been published in *PEN America* and is currently a finalist for *DoubleTake*'s upcoming 25 and Under.

**Richard Prince** lives in New York City and his work has been featured in numerous solo and group exhibitions.

**Andy Ryan** moved to New York from Phoenix two years ago. The two images included here are part of a body of work in progress for the last three years.

**Julie Reid** is the current editor of Sonoma State University's literary journal, *zaum*. Some of her other poems have appeared in *Lungfull!* magazine and *The Montserrat Review*.

**Ravi Shankar** recently graduated from Columbia University's MFA program. He has published poems in *The Paris Review*, *Gulf Coast*, *LIT*, *The Massachusetts Review*, *Descant* and *The Western Humanities Review*, and has held fellowships at Ragdale and the Atlantic Center for the Arts. He has worked as a teacher, bartender, copy-editor, knife salesman and instigator. He currently teaches English at Queens College and is the editor of *www.drunkenboat.com*. He does not play the sitar.

**Hugh Steinberg**'s poetry has appeared in *Grand Street*, *vert*, *American Poetry Review* and *Seneca Review*. He received an MFA from the University of Arizona in 1993, and recently completed a Wallace Stegner Fellowship at Stanford University. He teaches at the California College of Arts and Crafts, and is the recipient of a NEA creative writing fellowship for 2001-2002 in poetry. He lives in San Francisco.

**Virgil Suárez** was born in Cuba in 1962. Since 1974 he has lived in the United States. He is the author of over 20 books of prose and poetry, most recently of the collections *Palm Crows* (Univ. of Arizona Press) and *Banyan* (LSU Press). He divides his time between Miami and Tallahassee where he lives with his family and teaches creative writing at FSU.

**Matthew Thorburn** won the 2000 *Mississippi Review* Prize for poetry. His work has appeared, or is slated to appear, in *American Poetry Review*, *Seneca Review*, *Indiana Review* and elsewhere. He lives in New York City.

**Timothy Westmoreland** taught austronomy at the University of Texas at Arlington before completing his MFA at the University of Massachusetts at Amherst. His fiction has appeared in *Indiana Review*, *Quarterly West*, and *Best New American Voices 2001*. His first collection of short stories, *Good as Any*, is forthcoming from Harcourt in January 2002, and his first novel, *The Gathering*, will be published the following Fall.

**Marina Wilson** is originally from northern California and currently lives in New York City. Her previous publications include the *Berkeley Fiction Review* and *Poetry for the People Press*.

# THE PARIS REVIEW

Ernest Hemingway  E.M. Forster  Vladimir Nabokov  Norman Mailer
Allen Ginsberg  Italo Calvino  T.S. Eliot  Rick Bass  Dorothy Parker
John Updike  James Merrill  William Faulkner  Elizabeth Bishop
Tennessee Williams  Robert Bly  Lillian Hellman  T.C. Boyle  Sam
Shepard  Anne Sexton  James Baldwin  Arthur Miller  Don DeLillo
Harold Bloom  Robert Frost  Neil  P.L. Travers  Thornton Wilder
Jeffrey Eugenides  William  Shelby  Foote  Jean Cocteau  William
Carlos Williams  Geoffrey  Beauvoir  Martin McDonaugh
John Dos Passos  Graha  Burroughs  Philip Roth
Rebecca West  Mark Stra  de Carré  Frank O'Hara
Gabriel Garcia Marquez  Wendy  Berstein  E.L. Doctorow  Margaret
Atwood  Eugéne Ionesco  Ezra  Toni Morrison  Iris Murdoch
Raymond Carver  John Hollande  in Robbe-Grillet  Philip Larkin
August Wilson  V.S. Naipaul  José Saramago  John Ashbery  Terry
Southern  Günter Grass  Martin Amis  Milan Kundera  Joan Didion  Jack
Kerouac  Octavio Paz  Donald Hall  Tom Wolfe  Peter Matthiessen  John
Guare  Marianne Moore  Ken Kesey  John Irving  Kurt Vonnegut  Pablo
Neruda  John Cheever  Tom Stoppard  Jim Carroll  David Mamet  W.H.
Auden  Harold Pinter  A.R. Ammons  Denis Johnson  Rick Moody

## SINCE 1953

www.theparisreview.com  •  212.741.2365  •  distributed by Eastern News

MY

MISSPENT

YOUTH

Essays by
MEGHAN DAUM

**OPEN CITY** BOOKS

# POST ROAD

## PREMIERE

✱ photography by Catherine Athenien
✱ fiction by Gary Lutz | Maile Chapman | Kelcey Nichols
✱ poetry by Mark Bibbins | Nick Flynn | Kathy Nilsson | Larissa Szporluk
　　　Karen Volkman | C. Dale Young
✱ nonfiction by Joyce Lombardi | Gail Hosking Gilberg | David Manning
✱ Rick Moody on Montaigne | Douglas Bauer on Keith Scribner | Austin Flint on
　　　Eeva-Liisa Manner | Amy Hempel on Pearson Marx | A Letter from Sven
　　　Birkerts | A Postcard from E. Annie Proulx
✱ from the Post Road Archive: F. Scott Fitzgerald's Great Gatsby Contract
✱ Marty Fluger, Dawn Williams & Rocco van Loenen on The Grand Guignol

## ISSUE 2

### ✱ CONTRIBUTORS ✱

Pablo Medina | Dawn Raffel | Will Eno | Ambrose Bierce | Naomi Shihab Nye

David Shields | Jonathan Ames | Martha Cooley | Ken Kalfus | Ivan Klima | David Lehman

Tom Paine | Victoria Redel | Jim Shepard | Charles Wright | Charles Yoder

✱ Spring 2001 ✱

SUBSCRIPTIONS | $16/yr.
853 broadway suite 1516
new york ny 10003
212.780.3444
http://aboutface.org

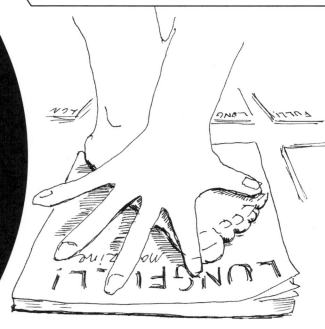

# goodfoot
## a poetry magazine

issue .1 spring .01

submissions
subscriptions

box 681
murray hill station
ny/ny 10156
goodfooted@hotmail.com

# BRIDGE
## STORIES AND IDEAS

ISSUE NUMBER THREE

Art Shay, John Barth, Vince Darmody, LD Beghtol, Rebecca Wolff, Patrick Welch, Wislawa Szymborska, Cris Mazza, Jim Munroe, Negativland, Gary Pike, Mike Topp, John Keene, Jon Langford, Frances Sherwood, Tim W. Brown, Mike Newirth, Wayne C. Booth, Lawrence Krauser

WWW.BRIDGEMAGAZINE.ORG

# 3rd bed

The individual pieces published in <u>3rd bed</u>, it goes without saying, are always surprising, stunningly original, and constantly testing all kinds of generic boundaries and conventions. But what I really admire is the manner in which the editors orchestrate this rich confusion. Without being thematic, <u>3rd bed</u> always has a thread—part Kevlar, part silk, part vein.

—Michael Martone

Beautifully designed and with an equal commitment to Shaker Mysticism, Ultraism, Dada, and contemporary innovative writing, <u>3rd bed</u> is eccentric and original. It works against the lock-step fake radicality of other magazines to give a home to genuinely edgy work.

—Brian Evenson

<u>3rd bed</u> is an essential, beautiful, and right-headed magazine, which is publishing some of the edgiest and most daring writers of our time.

—George Saunders

subscriptions:
$10.00 (two issues)

please send all queries to
<u>3rd bed</u>
17 union ave.,
jamaica plain,
ma 02130
or through
our website:
www.3rdbed.com

retailers:
<u>3rd bed</u>
is distributed by
small changes,
spd, and
bernhard deboer